# GREENWICH AT WORK

## PEOPLE AND INDUSTRIES THROUGH THE YEARS

DAVID C. RAMZAN

AMBERLEY

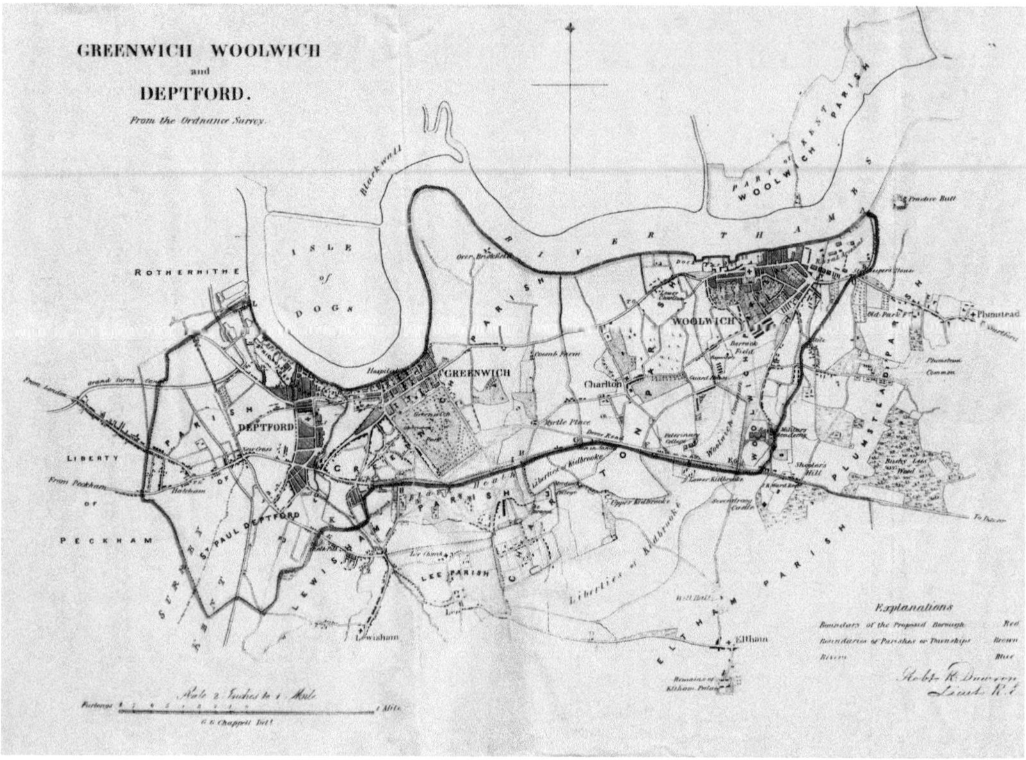


The parishes of Greenwich, Deptford and Woolwich, *c.* 1832, areas contributing to Greenwich at work.

*I should like to dedicate this publication to my ancestors whose lives were intertwined with working Greenwich, along with many friends and their own family members who, at one time, were employed in various workplaces and industries located within the borough, including Deptford to the west, through to Greenwich and Woolwich in the east.*


First published 2020

Amberley Publishing
The Hill, Stroud
Gloucestershire, GL5 4EP

www.amberley-books.com





ISBN 978 1 4456 9702 4 (print)
ISBN 978 1 4456 9703 1 (ebook)





British Library Cataloguing in Publication Data.
A catalogue record for this book is available from the British Library.

Origination by Amberley Publishing.
Printed in the UK.

# CONTENTS

# INTRODUCTION

## FROM A SMALL FISHING HAMLET TO A CENTRE OF MERCANTILE AND INDUSTRIAL COMMERCE

Standing at the riverside on the Isle of Dogs today, people looking out across the River Thames will see a panoramic view of Greenwich as the tidal water flows past the historic maritime town from the source in a Gloucester meadow, Trewsbury Mead.

At one time this ancient river was the busiest waterway in the world; however, the Thames at Greenwich today is devoid of almost all commercial craft, coastal vessels and shipping. Most of the old wharfs, warehouses, jetties and industrial sites have been demolished to make way for new property developments, including residential housing and luxury apartments, leisure facilities and hotels. Although a few tugs can still be seen towing lighters (barges) along the river, and on

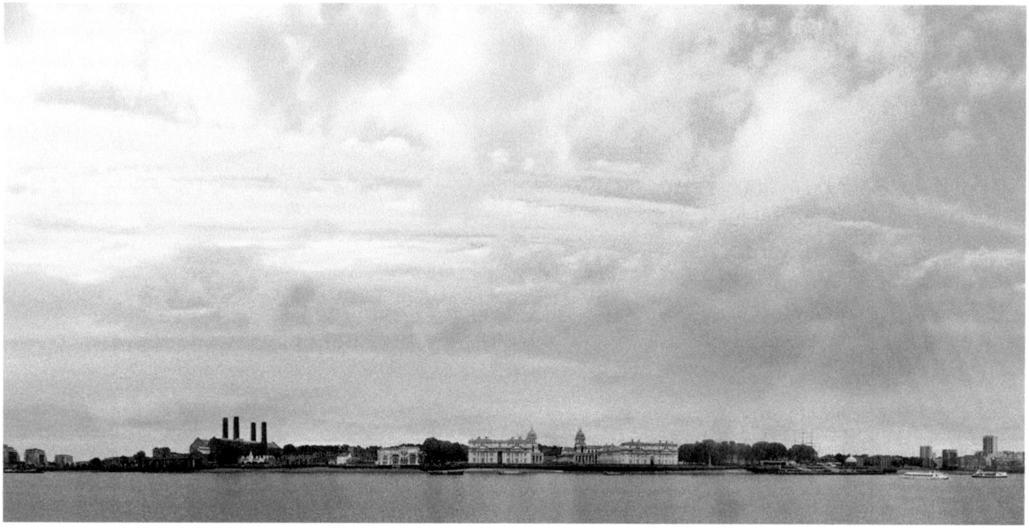

Greenwich from the Isle of Dogs, early twenty-first century, very different from when the riverside town was the centre of mercantile trade, industry and shipbuilding.

occasion you may be lucky to find a cruise liner or naval vessel moored at Greenwich Reach opposite Greenwich Pier, the majority of traffic at this point on the Thames consists of pleasure boats and fast Thames Clippers transporting commuters and tourists up and down the river.

First permanently settled by a small group of Anglo-Saxons, Greenwich, or *Gronewic* as the place was recorded in the Saxon charter of AD 918, meaning the 'green settlement', evolved over a period of a thousand years, into an important centre of mercantile and industrial trade and commerce.

Recorded in the 1086 Domesday Book as a settlement with a population of thirty-four households, Greenwich, then in the county of Kent, was placed in the 40 per cent of largest settlements listed. Under Tenant-in-chief Bishop Odo of Bayeux, half-brother to William I, the land, population and resources of Greenwich included ploughland consisting of two lord's plough teams, four men's plough teams, 22 acres of meadows, ten woodland swine render, four mills, twenty-four villagers, four smallholdings, one cottager and five slaves.

In modern times, Greenwich is more well known as a Royal Borough and World Heritage Site, with associations to royalty dating back to the time of Alfred the Great. Today's visitors and tourists are attracted to Greenwich to view the impressive places of historical interest including the Old Royal Naval College, the National Maritime Museum, the Old Royal Observatory and St Alfege Church. The Anglican parish church is the third place of worship built on the site where in 1011, the Archbishop of Canterbury, Alfege, was killed by Danish raiders after being kidnapped and brought to their Greenwich encampment. After his martyrdom, Greenwich became an important Christian place of pilgrimage.

These famous buildings, visited by tourists from all around the globe, have origins associated with Greenwich at work. The Old Royal Naval College, erected on the remnants of a royal palace, once the residence of kings and queens, was established as a hospital (almshouse and infirmary) for Britain's retired and injured naval seamen, and the National Maritime Museum, formerly the buildings of the Royal Hospital School, were first in use to educate boys in the skills of seamanship, leading to a career at sea, and to teach and train household duties to girls, to prepare them for work in domestic service.

The Old Royal Observatory, built on the site of Greenwich Castle, was central to the development of accurate astronomical navigation at sea, aiding Britain's trading and explorational voyages around the globe. The parish church of Greenwich, St Alfege, tended to the religious needs of all the town's parishioners, the working class, nobility and royalty.

At one time, shipbuilding had been of major importance to the Royal Borough's economy, where Henry VII first established a ship repair yard at West Greenwich, now known as Deptford. His son, Henry VIII, after being crowned king, converted the yard into a royal shipbuilding dockyard. The Tudor monarch then transformed a waterside wharf at Woolwich, to the east, once a place for trading wool, into another royal dockyard, specifically to build the Carrick warship *Henry Grace à Dieu*, known as the *Great Harry*, in honour of his father. The dockyard at Woolwich adjoined a large military establishment, the Royal Arsenal, where guns and ammunitions were manufactured, all three sites employing thousands of tradesmen and labourers, military and civilian.

To complement the shipbuilding industry, a substantial projection of land, Greenwich Marsh, enclosed by an upwards loop in the river, evolved from a barren marsh where sheep and cattle grazed, into an important area of commercial industrial establishments and boat and shipbuilding yards.

Through the expansion of manufacturing and maritime and riverside trades, along with the many industrial works stretching out along the riverside frontage from Deptford to Woolwich and across the whole of Greenwich Marsh, a vast number of people travelled to Greenwich to take up the many employment opportunities created. This resulted in the building of hundreds of blocks and rows of terraced housing throughout the borough, to accommodate new workers and their families.

The leafy suburban area located towards the south of Greenwich Park, from Blackheath Hill and onwards towards Shooters Hill, larger and more spacious properties were built, residencies of entrepreneurs, a majority whose wealth came through ventures in the mercantile trades, industry, commerce and banking.

# ANCESTRAL WORKERS

During the early years of my life, while living in a predominantly working-class area of Greenwich, it was difficult to fully appreciate the significance of the early working practices of Greenwich and how these helped to shape my hometown. Of course, everyone who lived in the local area were very well aware of the important role the Maritime Museum, Royal Naval College and Royal Observatory played in making Greenwich, literally, the centre of the world, the Meridian Line, 0° Longitude, passing centrally through the riverside town; however, by the late 1900s, Greenwich was about to move toward permanent whole-scale change.

The shipbuilding industries of Lower Thameside, at one time the largest in the world, had long since gone, although a few small boatbuilding yards and boat-repair yards remained, and the royal dockyards at Deptford and Woolwich, after closure and later suffering bomb damage during the Second World War, were gradually transforming into massive housing developments. The majority of historic industrial sites along the river and across Greenwich Marsh, later renamed Greenwich Peninsula, were steadily being swept away during a programme of regeneration, to make way for modern apartments, leisure facilities, hotels, entertainment venues, restaurants, bars and shopping centres.

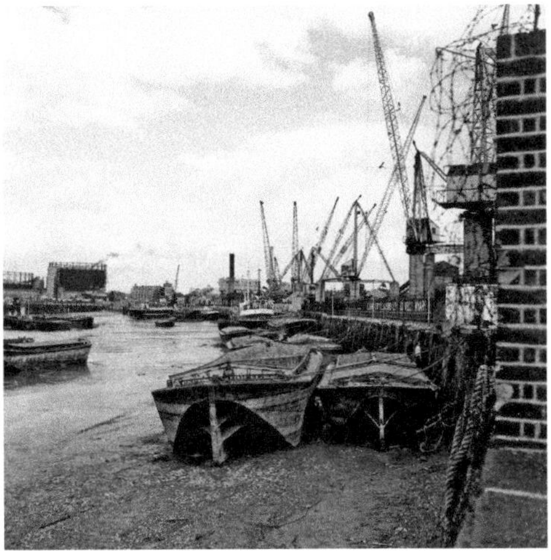

East Greenwich's working riverside, *c.* 1950, before regeneration. (Greenwich Heritage Centre)

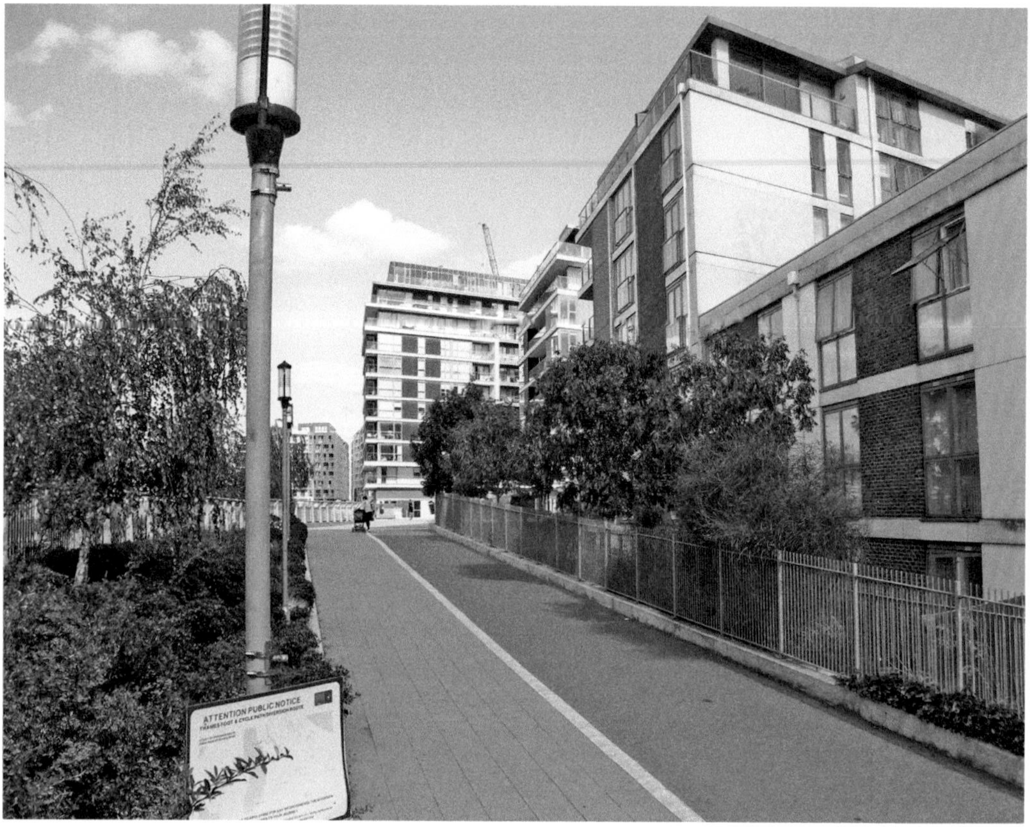


East Greenwich riverside, cranes and wharfs replaced by apartments, restaurants and bars.

Where at one time people worked and resided in their local surroundings, family members living in close proximity to each other, in society today, it is not unusual for work and home life to be located many miles apart. Family members move on, and away from their places of birth, and in this modern era, not only has the working landscape of Greenwich changed beyond all recognition, so has the town's working practices.

For my part, a majority of my ancestral relations were born, raised, resided and employed in, or ran small businesses in, the local area. My paternal grandfather however, Charles Ramzan, during the early 1900s had journeyed to Greenwich all the way from Peshawar, situated on an important silk trade route running through the Khyber Pass, the town included within the British Indian Empire. Leaving the family silk and cloth trade behind, my grandfather joined the British Royal Navy, as a boy sailor, prior to the onset of localised uprisings, the beginnings of an independence movement across India.

After arriving in England, my grandfather served aboard the training ship HMS *Victory*, based at Portsmouth, before making his way to Greenwich, where both the Royal Naval College and Royal Hospital School were located. At the age of eighteen, he married a local girl, Lilian Pearce, whose family were long-time Greenwich residents, and on leaving the navy established his own business, selling and trading assorted goods and wares.

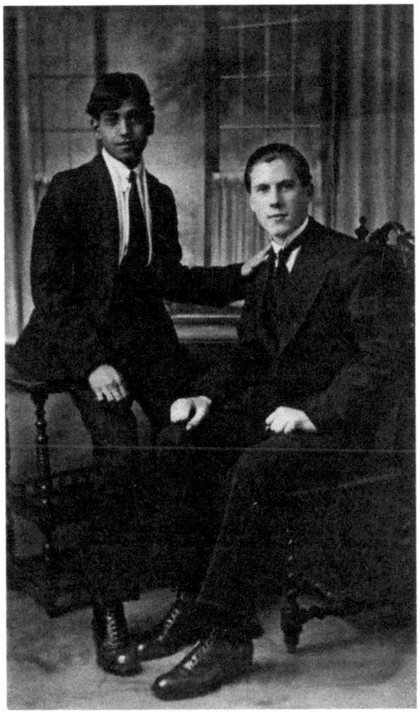

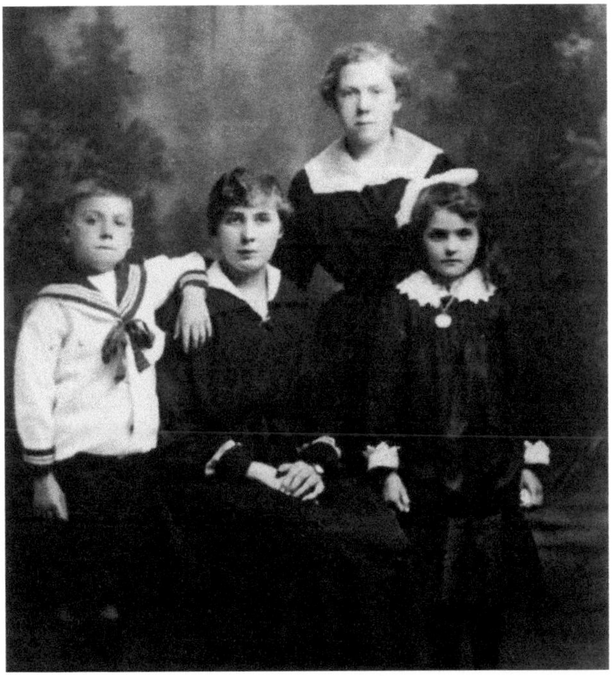

*Above left*: Charles Ramzan (left) with brother-in-law Ernie.

*Above right*: Lilian Pearce, my grandmother (seated), with two of her sisters, Kit and Betty, and younger brother Jim.

*Right*: The family home for over 100 years: No. 99 Old Woolwich Road, an early Victorian stuccoed terrace house, part of the Morden College Estate.

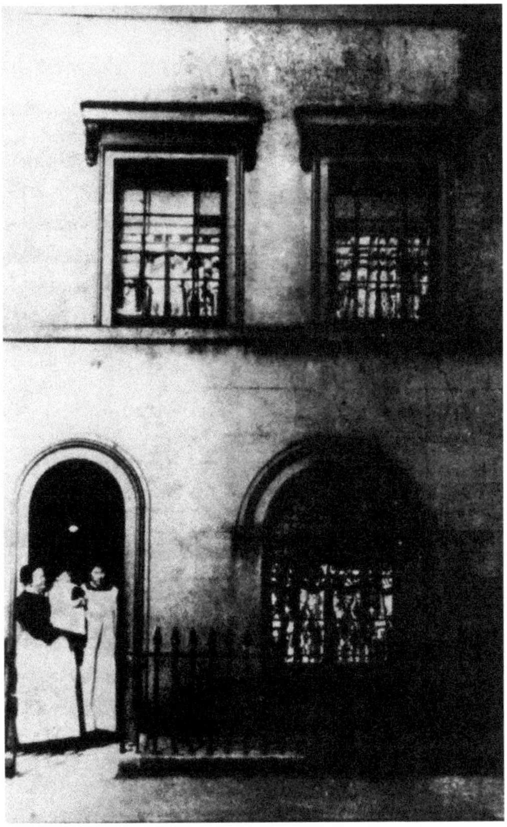

# TRADING PLACES

At the beginning of the 1900s, the profession and trade of Greenwich residents were recorded in the local census. Working women during this period were mostly employed as domestic servants, shopworkers, laundresses and, occasionally, innkeepers, a trade usually inherited by the widow of a licensee. The professions listed for males however, were much more varied. When my grandfather and grandmother moved into the family home at Old Woolwich Road after marriage, the occupations of their neighbours included a metal fitter, wharf clerk, tram driver, barge builder, marine store dealer, storekeeper, engineer's labourer, watchman, carpenter and a lighterman. Many of those workers had moved to Greenwich from other London parishes, some from other counties, and a few relocating from Wales, Ireland and Scotland.

On my mother's side of the family, my grandfather, Arthur Peachey, born and raised west of Greenwich at Deptford, was a descendant of the Angels, a fairly well-to-do family from Camberwell. After marrying my grandmother, Hanna Kerrison, who was of Irish descent, they moved into a typical working-class family terrace house east of Deptford Green, one of many properties erected during the 1800s to house dockyard and riverside industry workers. Arthur, or 'Buster' as my grandfather was known, drove lorries for a living and after the nationalisation of Britain's road haulage industry worked for British Road Services, one of the country's largest road hauliers, with a depot at Bermondsey and at Greenwich.

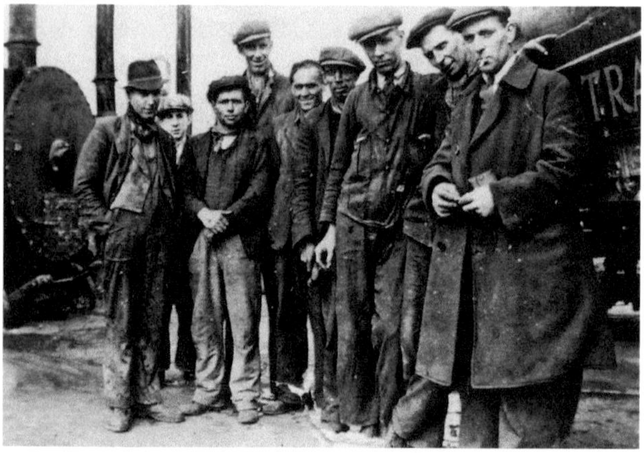

Far right: lorry driver Arthur Peachey, my grandfather, alongside his work colleagues from British Road Services.

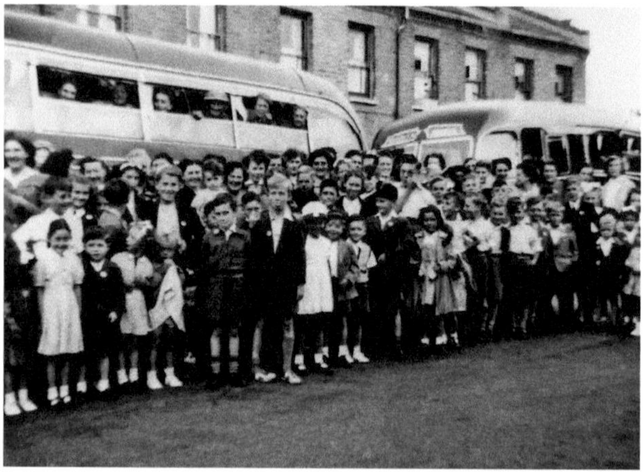

Coach outing to celebrate the coronation of Elizabeth II for residents of Staunton Street, Deptford, where my mother lived before marriage. My grandmother, Hanna Peachey, is second from the right on the coach.

# FAMILY WORKING PRACTICES

Most of my ancestors, up until the mid-1900s, would have worked in close proximity to the places where they lived, a time before improved transport systems and London's gradual expansion outwards provided workers opportunities to move to the suburbs and commute into work. On my father's side of the family, although a majority worked in various professions within the borough, the Robinson family line were much more adventurous.

Descendants of a military hereditary, one of my great-great uncles, William Robinson, joined the army to serve in China and India during a long-distinguished army career. William's brother John signed up with the Royal Navy and patrolled British-held waters to protect the country's interests around the globe aboard HMS *Cyclops*. Their younger brother Edward, a cabinetmaker by trade, who later became a police officer, set out to seek his fortune in Canada and then later the West Indies, after leaving the force.

My grandmother's father, Henry Pearce, worked as a handyman at Delta Metal Bronze & Brass Foundry on Blackwall Lane, Greenwich Marsh. One of her brothers, Jim Pearce, worked at Greenwich Power Station, situated on the riverfront, and another brother, Alfred, was employed by United Glass Bottle Works, east of Greenwich Marsh at Anchor and Hope Lane.

Although at the time when my Indian-born grandfather married my grandmother it would have been unusual for a man from India to be working and living in Greenwich, let alone taking up with and marrying a local English girl, many Lascars (Asian-born sailors) had already settled in the dockland areas of London since the seventeenth century. Employed by captains of merchant traders to man their ships on return voyages from the East Indies, when laid off after the ship made port, many Lascars made the decision not to return to sea, finding work, as well as wives, in the local area.

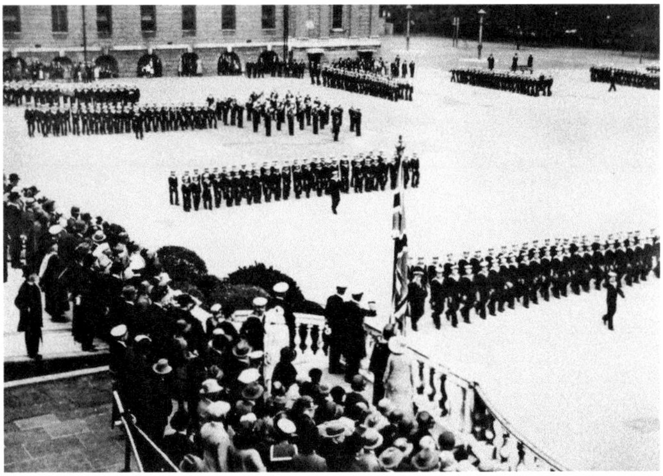

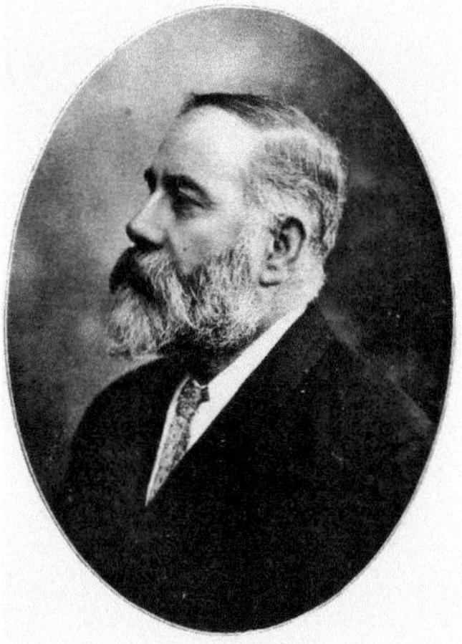

*Above left*: Some of the last boys to pass through the Royal Hospital School, where two of William Robinson's sons were educated, before the establishment relocated to Suffolk in 1933.

*Above right*: Edward Robinson in his later years – former Greenwich cabinetmaker, police officer and North America frontiersman.

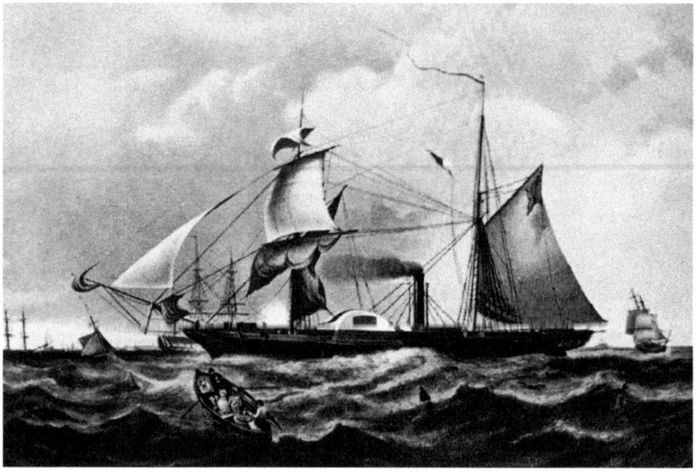

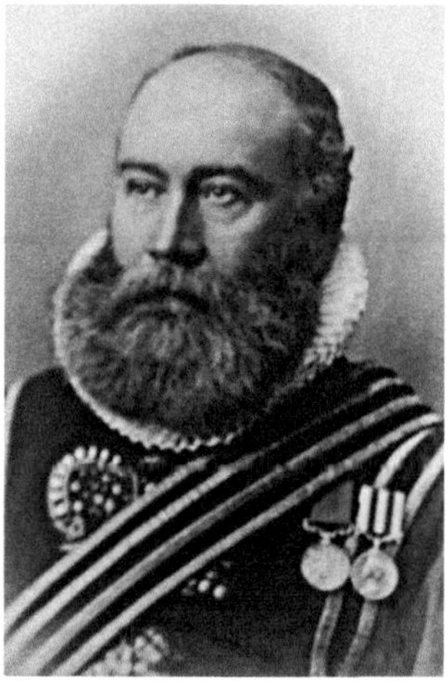

*Above left*: HMS *Cyclops*, John Robinson's Royal Navy paddle sloop.

*Above right*: William Robinson, who served in the British Army overseas until appointed to the Yeoman of the Guard in 1887. His duties included acting as bodyguard to Queen Victoria.

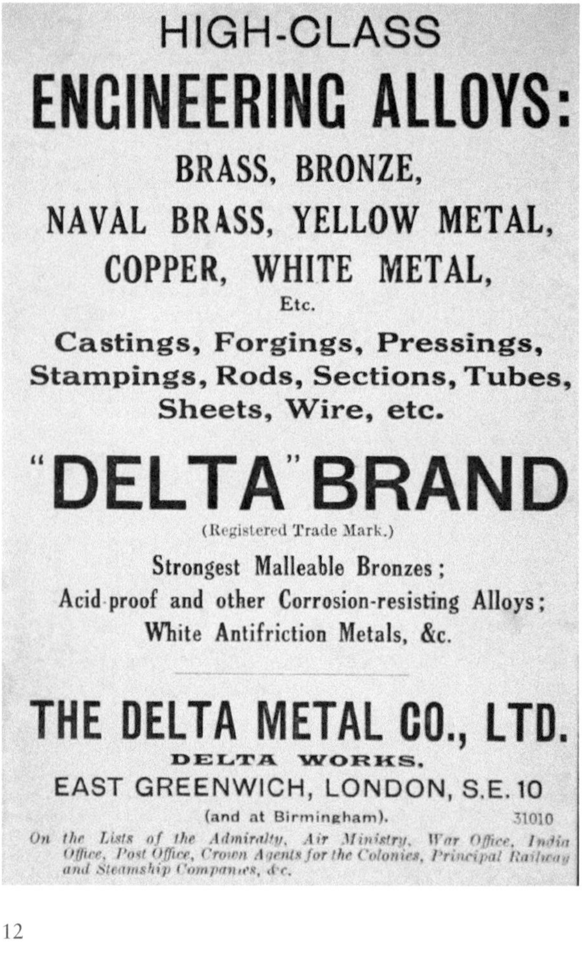


Advertisement for Delta Metal Works, East Greenwich.

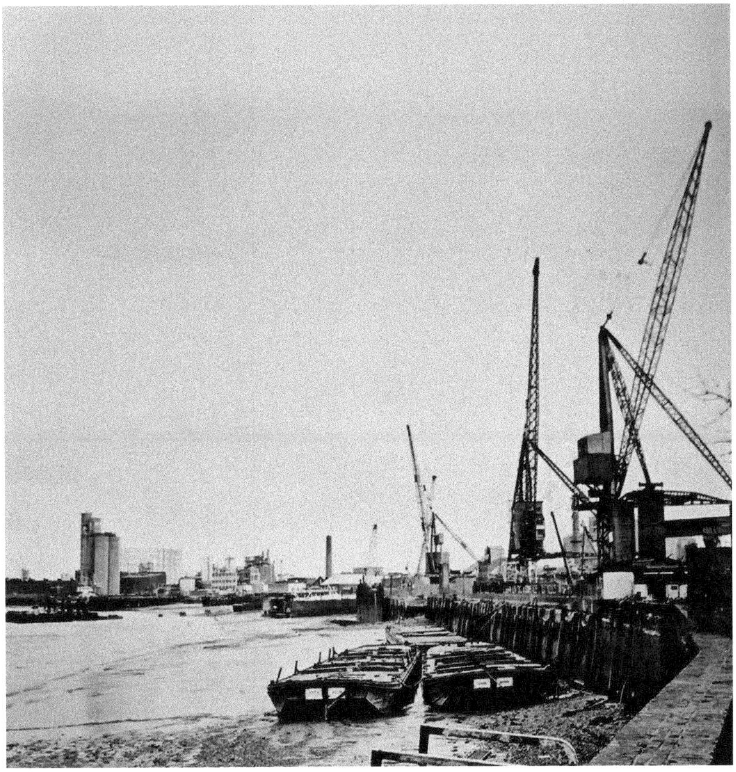

South bank of the working Thames from Lovell's Wharf to Greenwich Marsh. The riverside cranes were used to offload cargo from ships, boats, barges and lighters. (Greenwich Heritage Centre)

Some years after my grandfather died when only in his early forties, my grandmother married widower George Austin, who lived in the same street. George, or 'Pop' as he was referred to by the younger family members, had spent most of his working life as a lighterman on the river after leaving the army. He then worked as a crane operator offloading colliers arriving from north-east of England, a time when coal played an important part in the working history of Greenwich.

My father began his working career as an apprentice plumber, and after qualification, worked on many building projects across all of London. Later, a family friend offered him the opportunity to work as a car salesman at his dealership in Erith – a much cleaner job. Some years later he worked for a car showroom located on Trafalgar Road, Greenwich, selling cars to local workers, before joining the Co-op in his later years. On leaving education, my mother took up a position in clerical work, and after marriage was employed in the accounts office of a local furniture dealer, Kerr's, located on Greenwich High Road. When a new taxi service, Greenwich Mini Cabs, opened their office opposite our house on Old Woolwich Road, my mother successfully applied for the position as the minicab drivers' controller.

After several years taking telephone bookings and directing minicab drivers to pick up clients, my mother joined Greenwich Building Society, a very old and well-established local business founded in 1809. Greenwich Building Society was the first recorded London-based building society established for the purpose of raising funds by subscription and offering members advancements to purchase property through a mortgage repayable by instalments. This gave working-class people a chance to own their home rather than paying rent as a tenant to a landlord or housing association.

Members of my immediate family also worked locally in various retail positions and public services; however, as other employment opportunities presented themselves outside of the local area, and ownership of property became much more affordable beyond inner London, many relocated to the outer suburbs, as well as into Kent, myself included.

# ODD JOBS AROUND GREENWICH

While at secondary school, it was possible for youngsters like me to earn some extra pocket money carrying out odd jobs at weekends. I cycled around Greenwich on Sunday mornings delivering newspapers for two shillings a week, plus tips at Christmas, and then helped out on a greengrocer's stall on Saturdays. During the late 1960s, there were many market stalls selling a variety of goods situated on side streets leading off from Trafalgar Road, the main shopping area for East Greenwich, many stalls offering youngsters the chance of earning a bit of extra cash.

During the school summer break, I also had a part-time job working for the National Maritime Museum, serving in the visitors' café and Greenwich Park Tea Pavilion. On leaving education, I headed off to London where I began a career in design and advertising, commuting to and from my place of work by train, occasionally travelling by some more unusual modes of river transport: hovercraft and hydrofoils running from Greenwich Pier to London and back. Although hovercraft and hydrofoils have long since gone, commuters and tourists are now able to travel on sleek new Thames Clippers, a service which began operation at the beginning of the twenty-first century.

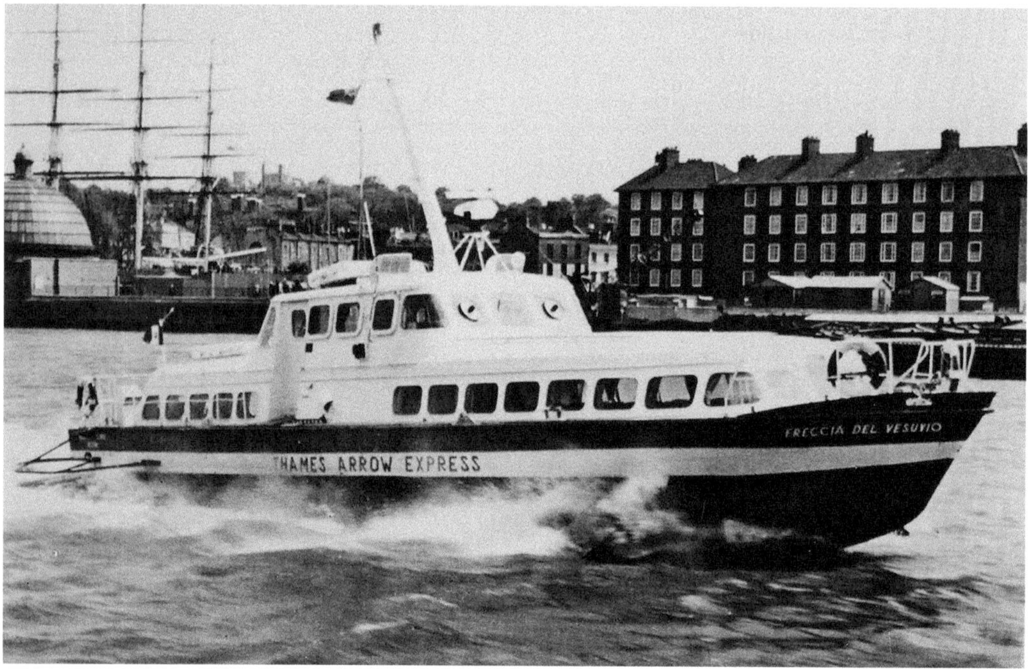


Thames Arrow Express hydrofoil, one of the ways commuters travelled on the river to and from Greenwich Pier during the early 1970s. (A. Phinbow)

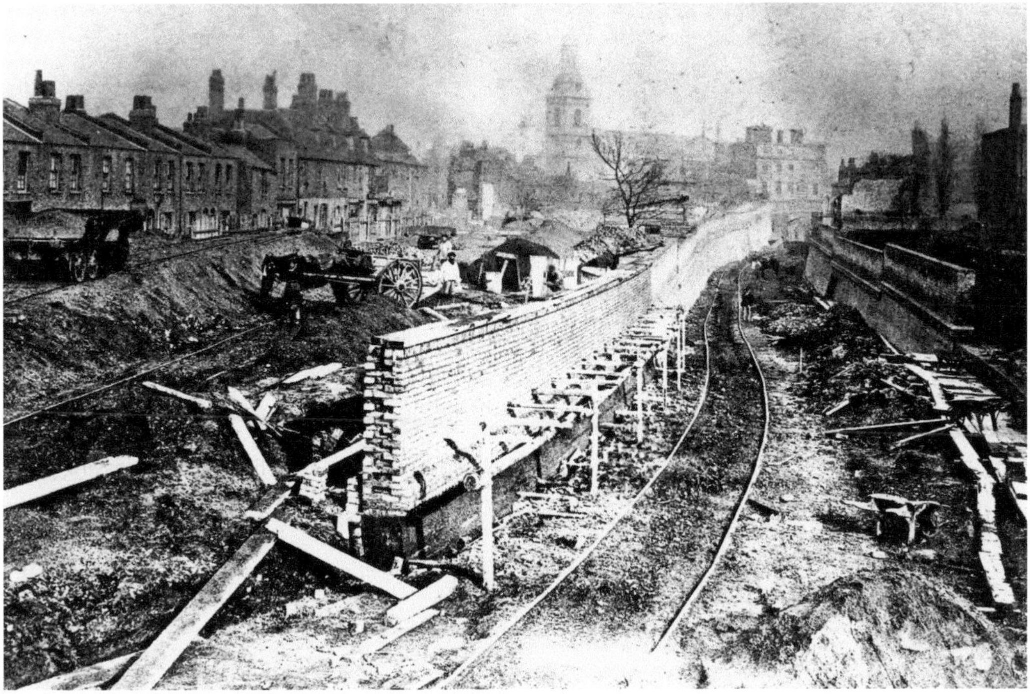

The building of rail line extension, *c.* 1870, from Greenwich Terminus towards East Greenwich, Woolwich and onwards into Kent.

# COAL AND GAS

A greater proportion of Greenwich's economy came through coal at the beginning of the Industrial Revolution, a major turning point in British and global history, and one of the first men who brought coal down from the North East to Greenwich was merchant William Coles Child. While still in his early twenties, after taking over the family coal wharf site on the Southbank of the Thames in London, Child acquired a site on Greenwich Marsh in 1838, from landowner's Morden College, a charitable institution, to expand the company's business dealings.

As part of the deal to lease the site, Child was required to carry out improvements to road access and land drainage. Working with Morden College, Child built a new housing estate running from Woolwich Road up towards the river, close to where his coal wharf was situated, erecting a public house, the Pelton Arms, named after Pelton Main, a County Durham colliery, at the end of a smart row of terrace houses.

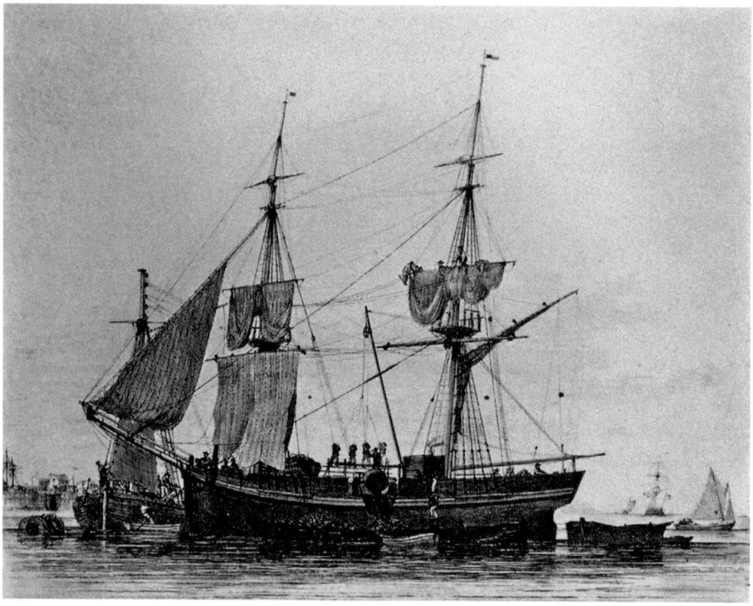

Early nineteenth-century collier offloading coal into a lighter at Woolwich.

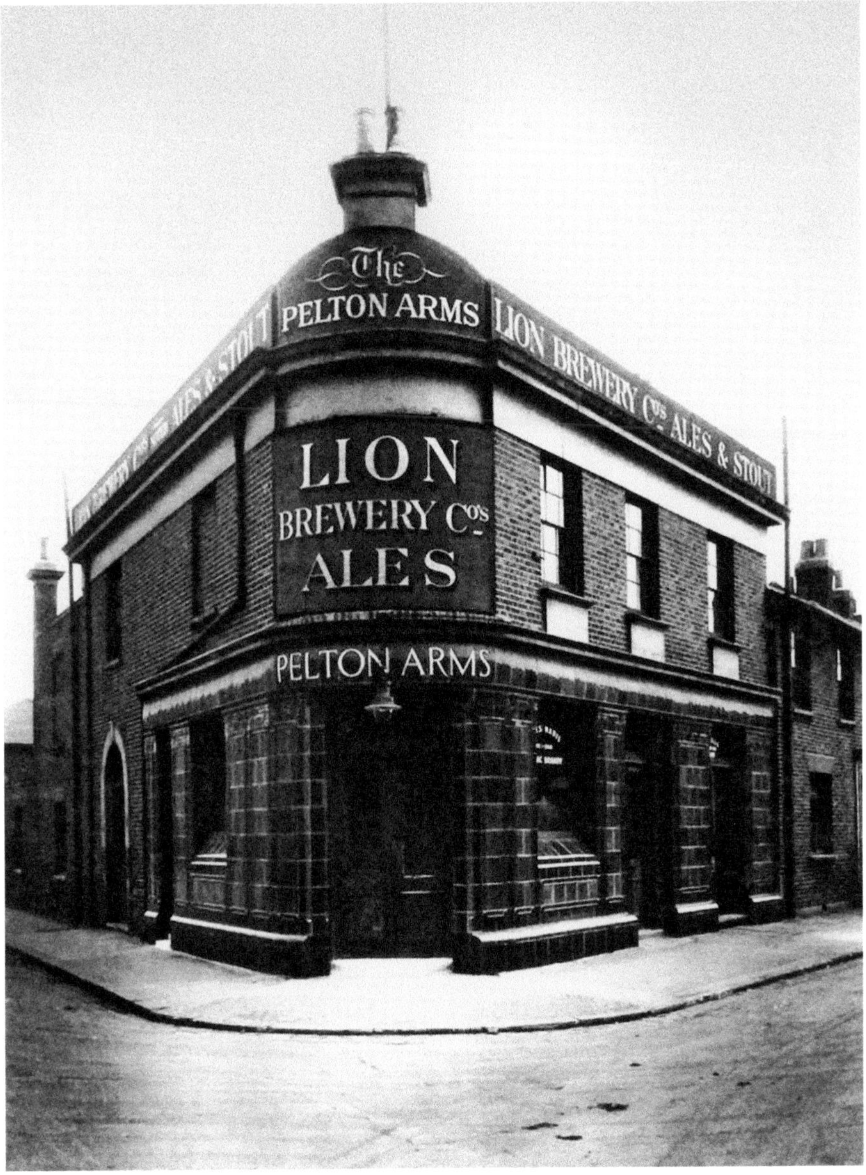


The Pelton Arms public house, erected towards the river end of Pelton Road in 1844.

The streets making up this new housing development were similarly named after places in the North East, including Newcastle Street and Pelton Road. Child also owned gravel pits and brick works at nearby Bromley and was soon dealing in cement and coal processing at Greenwich Wharf, where colliers were able to offload cargos of coal onto wagons for distribution directly to the railways, iron foundries and the many new industries along the river.

The collier traffic on the Thames was controlled by the Greenwich Harbour Master, from an office built in 1855 adjacent to Greenwich Wharf, later known as Lovells Wharf,

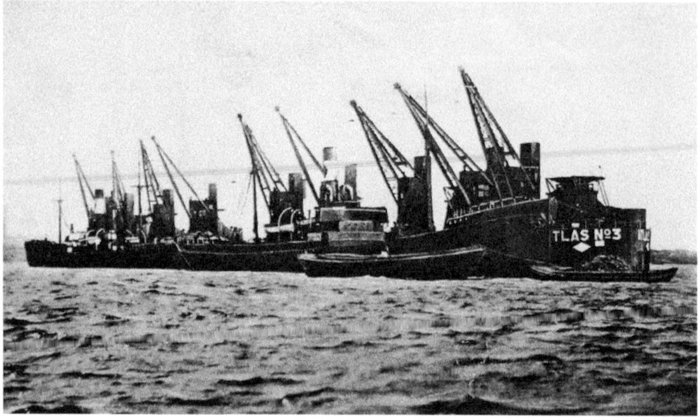

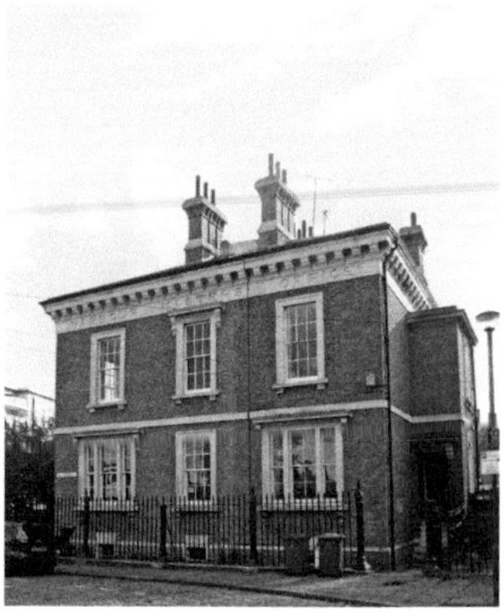

*Above left*: Floating derricks offloading coal from steam colliers moored at Woolwich Reach.

*Above right*: Harbour Master's Office, Ballast Quay, refurbished as a place of residence.

replacing an earlier harbour master's office located near the Yacht Tavern public house at Crane Street.

Colliers of various tonnage shipped coal to Greenwich not only to supply the railways and steam-powered industries, but also a succession of the borough's coal-fired power stations located at Deptford, Woolwich, Blackwall Point and Greenwich.

## POWER FOR THE PEOPLE

Commissioned and built around the turn of the nineteenth century, these important power stations, providing electricity for both industry and domestic use, became strategic targets in both World Wars. In the First World War, a Zeppelin dropped a bomb on the Deptford site, killing one worker, and during the Second World War, twenty-seven staff were killed in an air raid. Although suffering some bomb damage, all four power stations survived the war; however, after various alterations and additions over the following years, three were decommissioned and then demolished, Greenwich Power Station the only one left standing.

When Greenwich Power Station was built, enormous quantities of coal were required to fuel the massive boilers and a large jetty was constructed on the river's edge to offload coal directly from colliers then load coal residue onto lighters for disposal. The steam-powered engines were replaced by steam turbine alternators in 1922, which were superseded by more efficient oil-fuelled Rolls-Royce gas turbines. Currently, there are plans to install six new state-of-the-art gas turbines, providing low carbon energy to supply heat and hot water to local schools and homes, and electricity to power London's Tube system.

The amount of coal consumed by industry, homes and the railways during 1880s and early 1900s resulted in the increase of coal and coke arriving at Greenwich by collier and the growth of merchants dealing in coal, and an increase in wharfs and jetties for unloading this lucrative commodity.

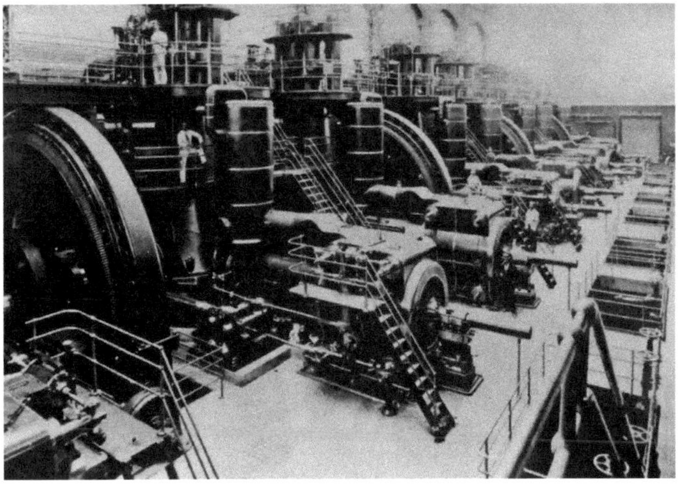

The power station's engine room, early 1900s, containing four massive steam engines driving flywheel alternators with an output of 6,600 volts (25 hertz).

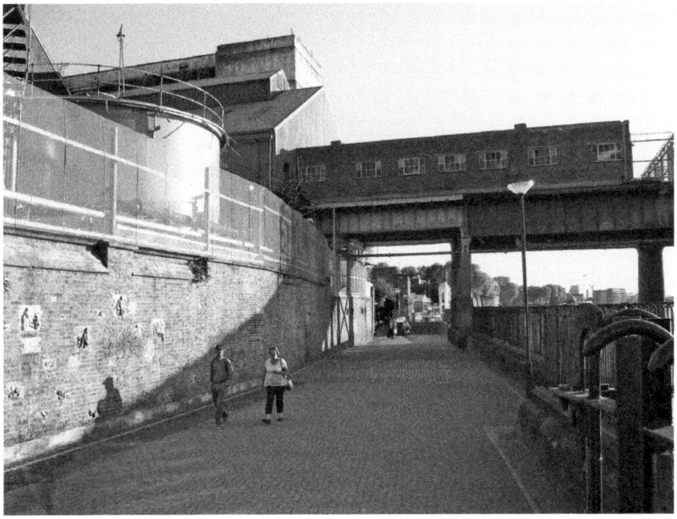

Riverside jetty overhead conveyor used to move coal directly into Greenwich Power Station.

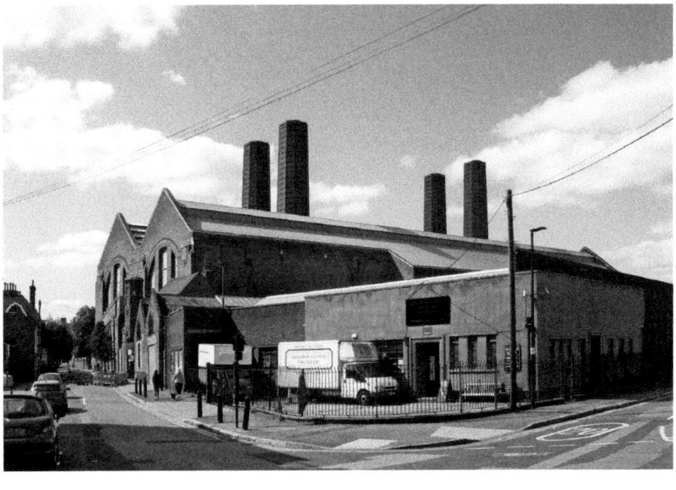

Greenwich Power Station, Old Woolwich Road, erected between 1902 and 1910.

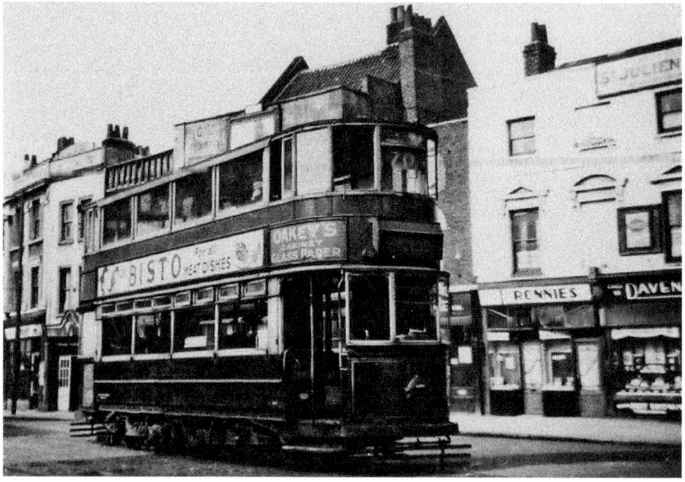


Electric tram, Greenwich Church Street, powered by electricity generated at Greenwich Power Station.

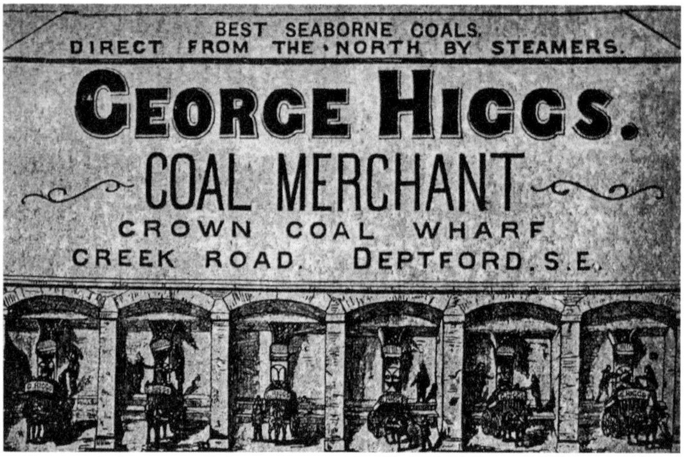


One of the coal merchants of Greenwich.

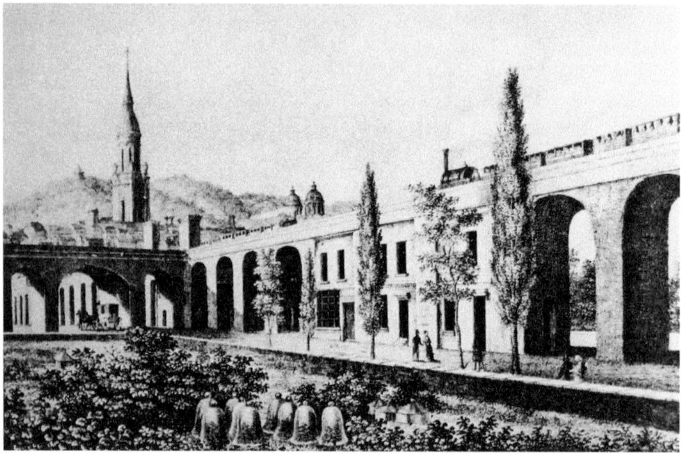

The viaduct built for the Greenwich steam passenger railway opened between 1836 and 1838.

# THE SUBSTANCE OF GAS

In the late 1800s, a small gas company, South Metropolitan, under the direction of chairman George Livesey, opened a 140-acre site on Greenwich Marsh to convert coal into gas. A huge gasometer was then constructed to hold the gas, at the time the largest in the world with a capacity of 8,600,000 cubic feet. The impressive iron-built structure, which could be seen from miles away, dominated the Greenwich Marsh industrial skyline. Unsurprisingly, many people who used the marsh for grazing livestock protested against their loss of right of way, which fell within the gasworks site, forcing contractors to provide a gang of men to stop their continued passage through.

An even larger holder with a capacity of 12,200,000 cubic feet was erected adjacent to the first, the Greenwich Gas Works becoming the largest and most progressive in the world. The company had a fleet of its own colliers for transporting coal from the north-east coalfields to meet the demand of the gasworks, and many subsidiary businesses surrounding the site.

Although the Greenwich Gas Works offered employment to hundreds of workers, a strike broke out in 1889, shortly after the formation of the unions, over the long shift hours staff

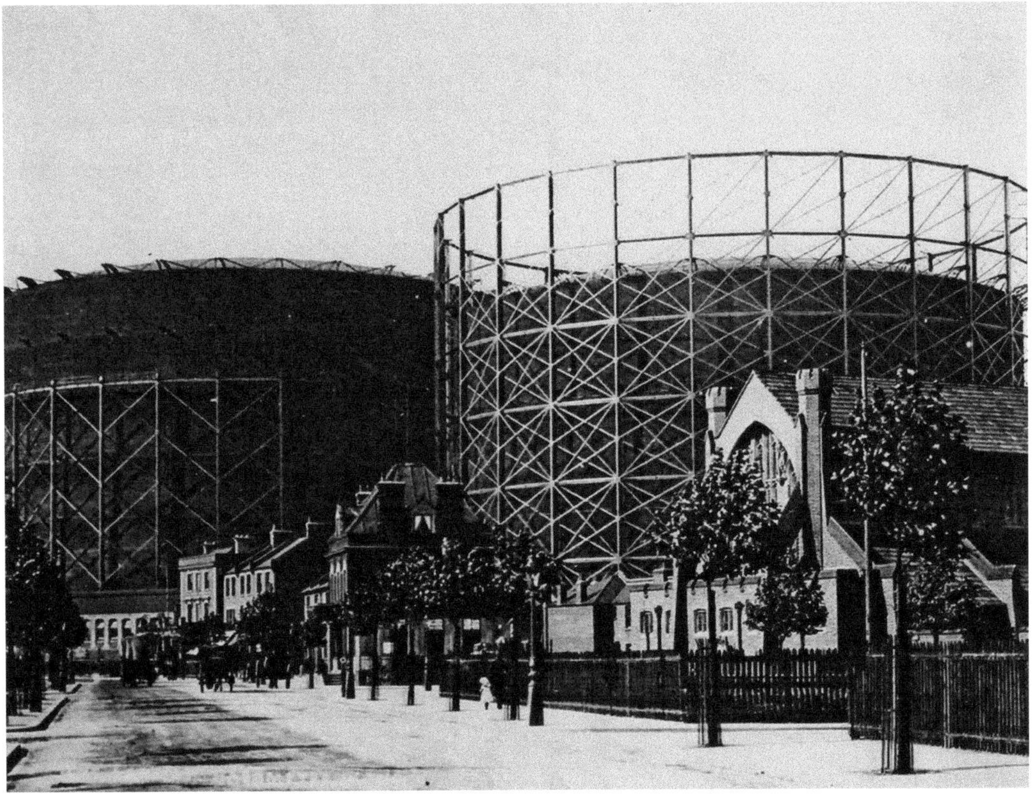

Greenwich Gasometers No. 1 and No. 2 stored gas to supply the borough's street lamps and industrial and domestic properties.

were required to work. Livseley brought in blackleg labourers to keep the works running, resulting in many regular employees losing their jobs. Eventually working practices improved and Greenwich Gas Works employees received various benefits above their wages, including medical healthcare, holiday schemes and leisure activities. Towards the end of the nineteenth century, East Greenwich Gas Works staff earned an average of £1.10 shillings a week, an equivalent of around £190 today.

In 1917, Gas Holder No. 1, the first to be erected, was damaged when an explosion occurred across the river at the Silvertown munitions factory, and during the Second World War, bombs dropped over the riverside industries also caused some damage to the site. After a bomb planted by the IRA exploded adjacent to both gasometers in 1979, seriously damaging Gas Holder No. 2, the gasometer was then demolished during the mid-1980s. When the gasworks site ceased production in 1976, after the introduction of North Sea gas, the lone surviving gasholder came under threat of demolition, as the regeneration of Greenwich Marsh progressed relentlessly, considered not worthy of preservation.

Other industrial sites connected to the gas works using coal by-products included a tar works at Ordinance Wharf, Thames Soap Works, and Bethell's, producing tar-soaked railway sleepers, telegraph poles and later, after the business became the Improved Wood Pavement Co., creosoted wooden blocks used for road paving and flooring.

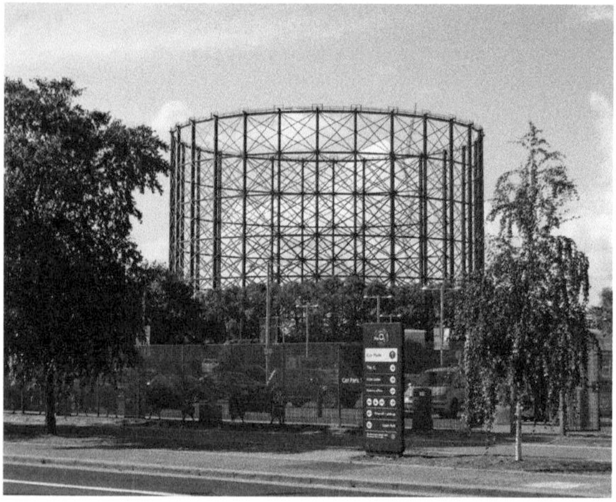

The framework of Gasometer No. 1 before dismantling began in early 2020.

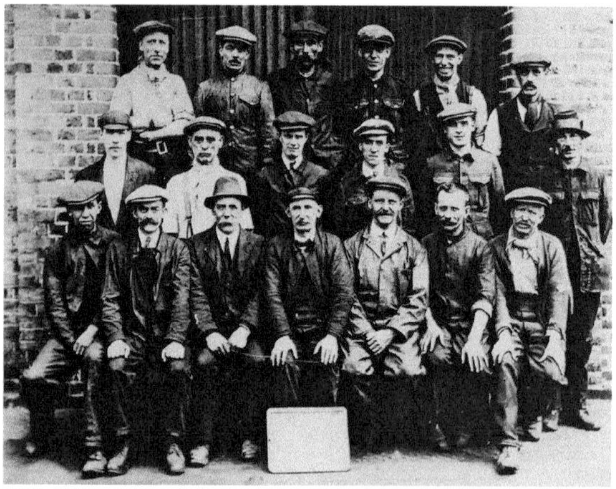

Gang of workers from East Greenwich Gasworks, c. 1920, one of the area's major employers with around 5,000 staff.

Coke, a carbonised coal and oil mixture, was also made at the gasworks, mainly used to fuel industrial furnaces, forges and stoves. Ammonia produced in the production of coke was made into fertiliser, and gas was also used to fuel various gasworks vehicles. Along with site workers, the gasworks employed roadwork labourers, gas maintenance staff, and laboratory specialist chemical processors to refine residue coal gas. The South Metropolitan Gas Company then opened a showroom at Powis Street, Woolwich, selling gas fittings, mantles, gas fires and stoves.

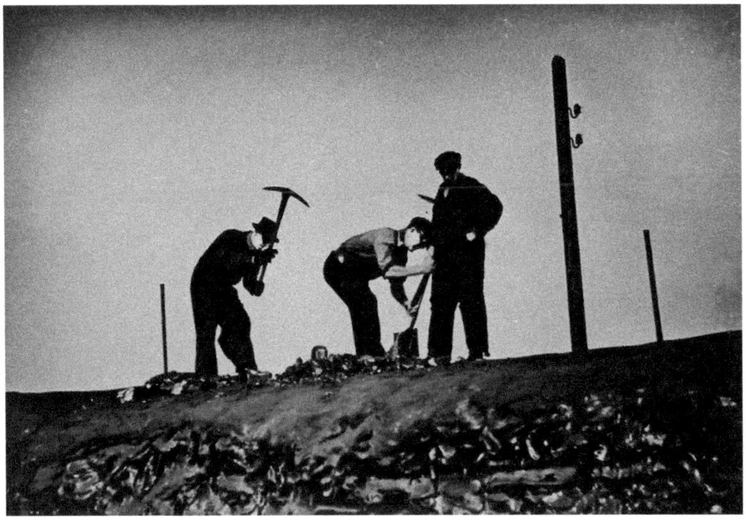

Tar and pitch labourers at Greenwich Marsh, early 1900s. Bethal's Tar & Chemicals Works was one industry connected with coal by-products. (Greenwich Heritage Centre)

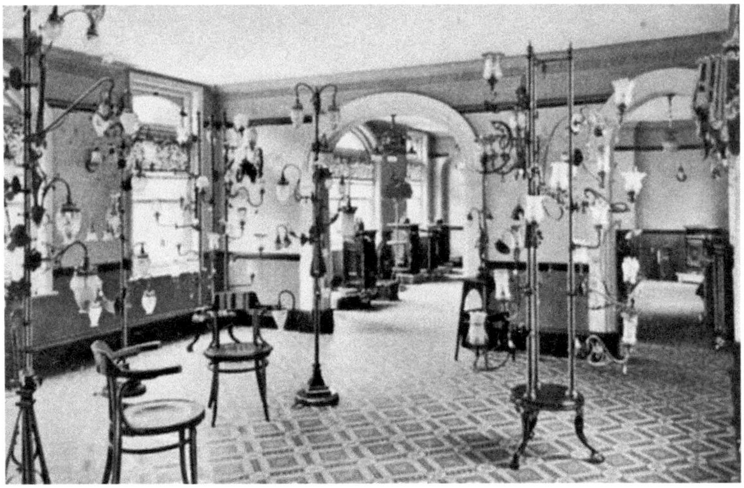

Gas showroom, Powis Street, Woolwich, selling various gas light fittings and appliances.

# ON THE MARSH

Industrial Greenwich included modern-day Greenwich Peninsula, historically known as Greenwich Level, which as the name implied was an open level area of land. The peninsula was shaped by an upwards loop in the Thames, the river forming the west, north and part of the eastern boundary, Lombarde's Wall, a flood barrier making up the remainder. To the south, the marsh was bordered by the main Greenwich to Woolwich thoroughfare. Up until the early 1600s, the marsh was mainly used for grazing livestock, with very few structures erected until the early 1800s.

## EXPLOSIVE BEGINNINGS

When Sir Christopher Wren received a commission to complete the building of the Royal Hospital on the site of Greenwich Palace, the gunpowder stored in a vacated palace building was moved to Greenwich Marsh for storage in a Board of Ordnance gunpowder magazine, originally an Elizabethan watchtower.

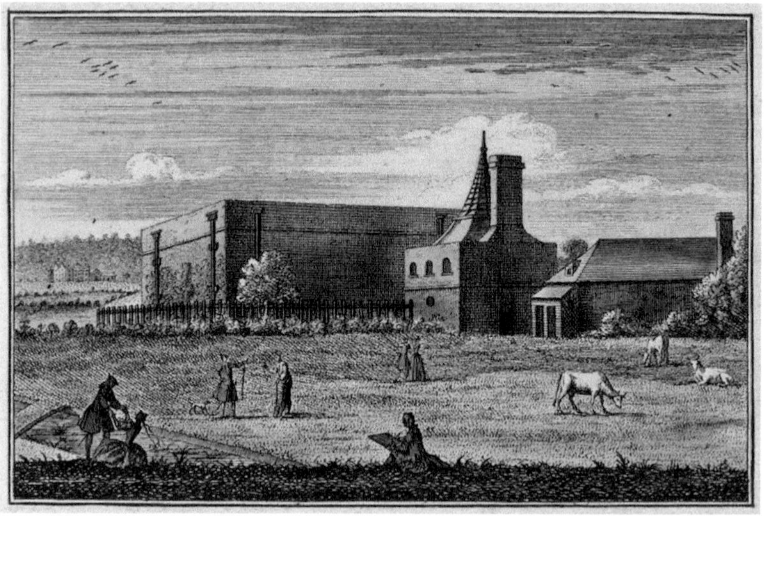

Gunpowder Magazine, c. 1738, erected close to present-day Enderby Wharf.

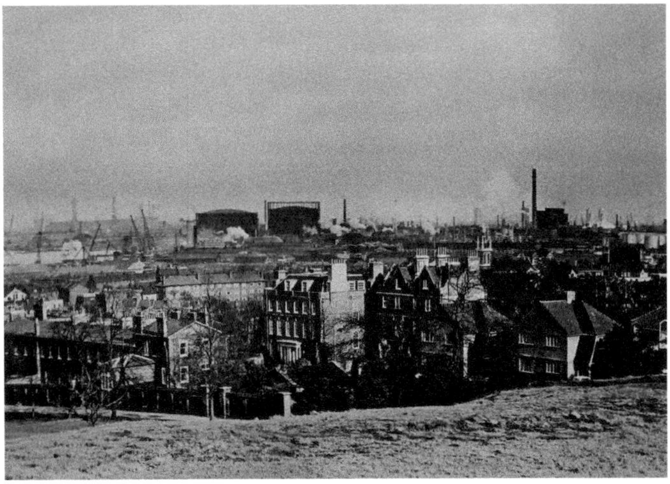

View from Greenwich Park of industrialised Greenwich Marsh, early 1900s.

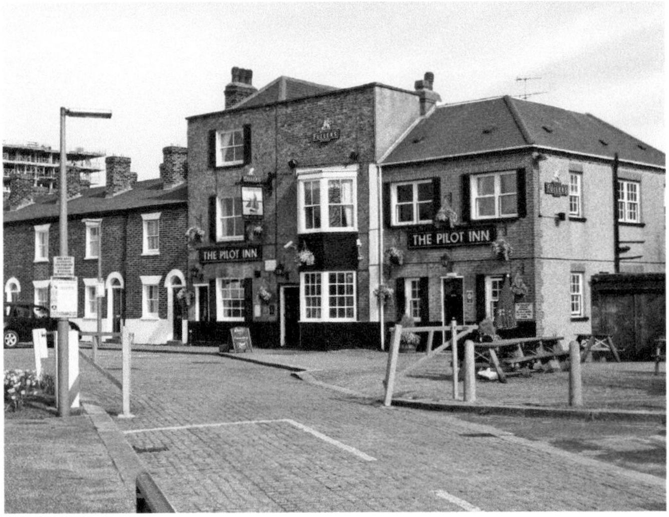


The Pilot, prior to refurbishments, built for workers of the new East Greenwich community.

By the mid-eighteenth century, the building was in such poor condition there were fears that if there was ever an explosion the blast could well destroy a majority of Greenwich, and a bill was passed to relocate the magazine to Purfleet on the Essex marshes.

A greater part of marsh land was owned by charitable organisations and with the coming of the industrial age, large areas were leased out for commercial development.

Opposite William Coles Child's coal wharf, to the east of the marsh, industrialist George Russell created New East Greenwich, consisting of a large corn tidal mill and a row of millworkers' terraced houses, Ceylon Place, with a public house, the Pilot, at the end. It has been suggested the public house acquired its name in reference to words of a song sung out at the inauguration of the Pitt Club, 'here's to the Pilot that Weathered the storm', a tribute to former Prime Minister William Pitt the Younger, who, along with his elder brother and several politicians, held leases on marsh land.

The Pilot, one of many marsh hostelries, was not only frequented by the millworkers but also by workers employed in the many other local industries.

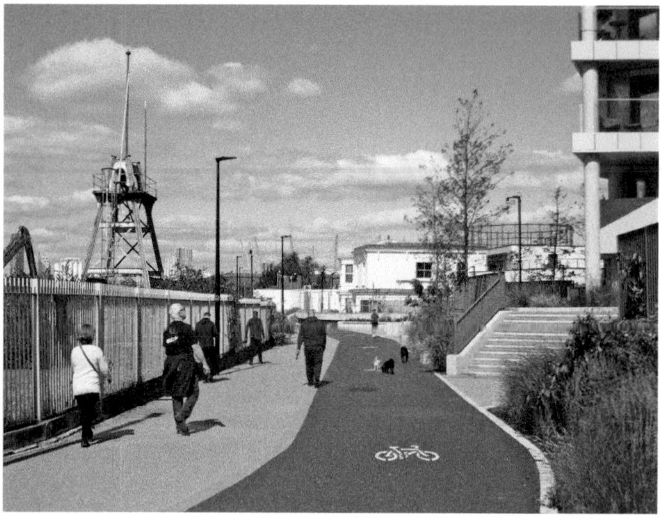

River walkway leading towards Enderby Wharf and the historic nineteenth-century Enderby House.

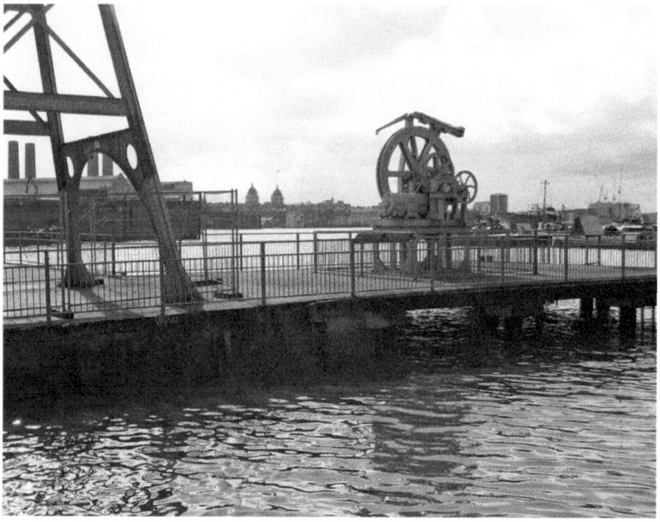

Enderby Wharf jetty, where subsea telegraph cable would have been loaded aboard cable ships by way of a gantry, bearer wire and pulley system.

## FROM WHALING TO TELEGRAPHY

To the west of Greenwich Marsh stands the unimposing, but historically important, Enderby House, a Grade II detached building once the residence of the Enderby family. Erected during the early nineteenth century, the house stood opposite a site acquired by Samuel Enderby II for the manufacture of rope and canvas to supply the family's whaling fleet. Enderby's operated sixty-eight ships, one of which, the *Amelia*, sailed west around Cape Horn in 1789, the first whaler to hunt whales in the Southern Ocean.

Enderby's became London's largest whaling company, employing a vast number of workers in both catching and processing whales. After funding several pioneering expeditions into the Southern Ocean, leading to the discovery of the Bellany Islands and the founding of the Enderby Settlement at Port Ross, north-east of the Auckland Islands, the financial investments

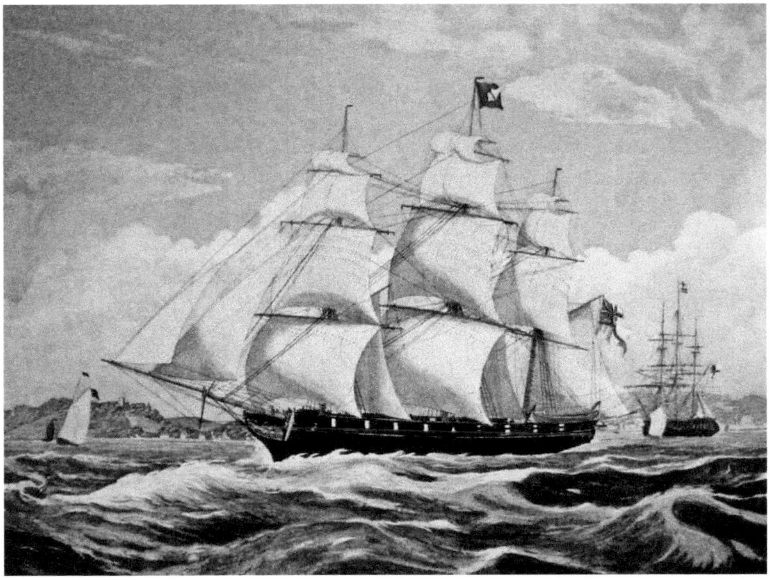

The *Samuel Enderby*, launched in 1834, one of a fleet of Enderby whaling ships.

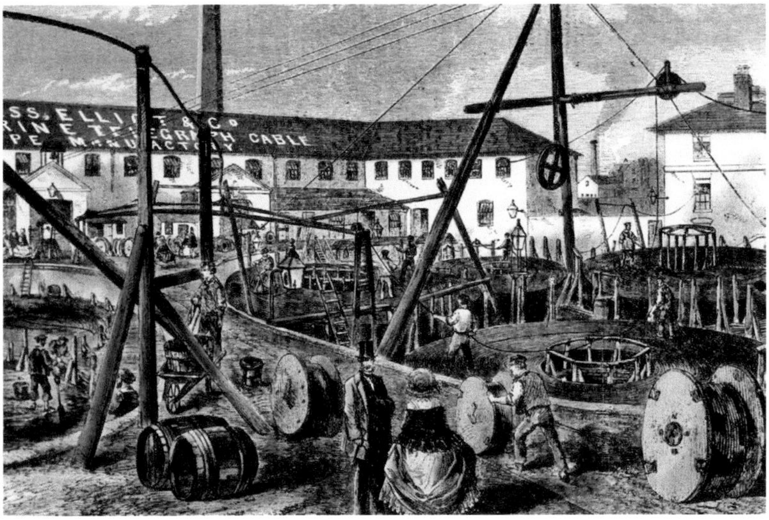


Glass, Elliott & Co.'s telegraph cable works, mid-nineteenth century.

made in the unproductive Enderby Settlement brought about the company's financial ruin and liquidation.

The Enderby site was sold to Glass, Elliott & Co., for the production of submarine telegraph communication cables, and the house was used as office space. Glass, Elliott & Co. merged with the Telegraph Construction and Maintenance Company, and went on to manufacture the very first subsea telegraph cable successfully laid between Britain and America. When part of the works was sold off for redevelopment, the Grade II listed Enderby House, along with the jetty and cable transfer machinery, were retained, a surviving reminder of the important role the Greenwich Marsh telegraph works played in the development of global communications.

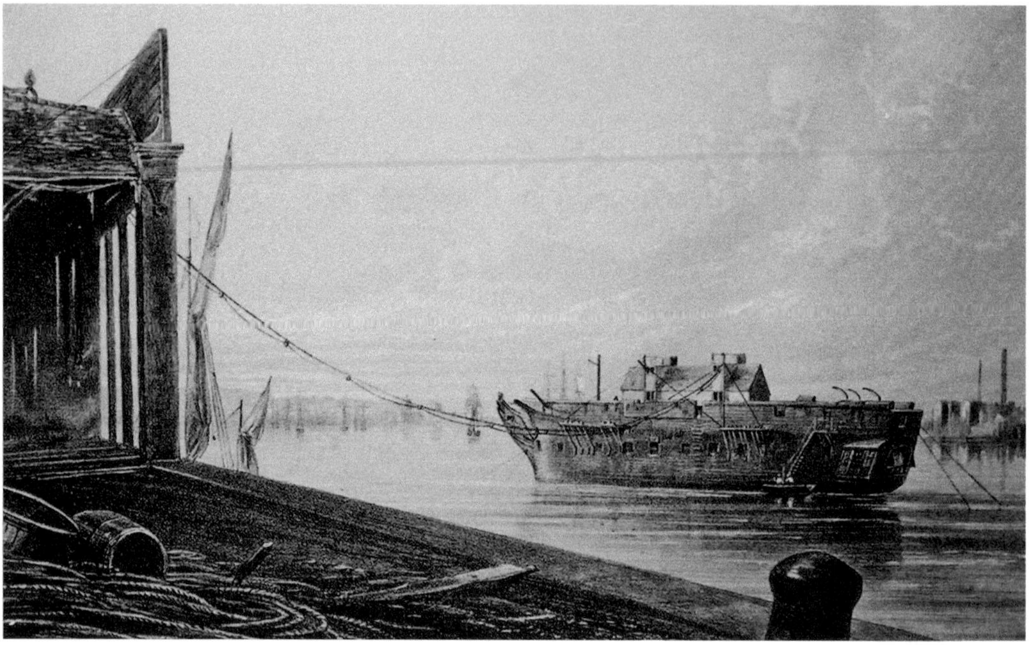

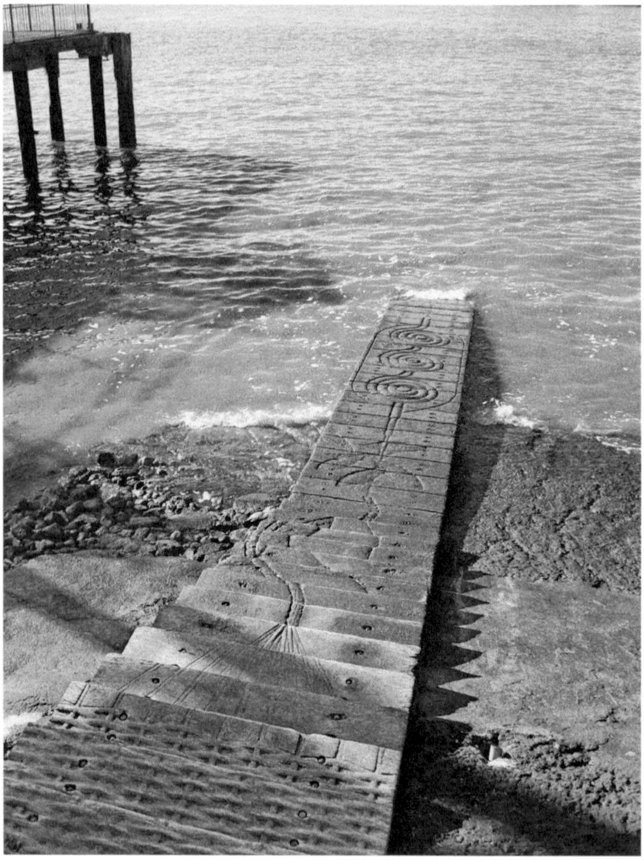

*Above*: Cable hulk *Amethyst* moored opposite Enderby Wharf, where cable was passed from the works onto the hulk, before being towed to cable layer *Great Eastern* at Sheerness.

*Left*: Enderby Wharf Ferry Steps, a contemporary wooden artwork depicting the marsh's industrial heritage.

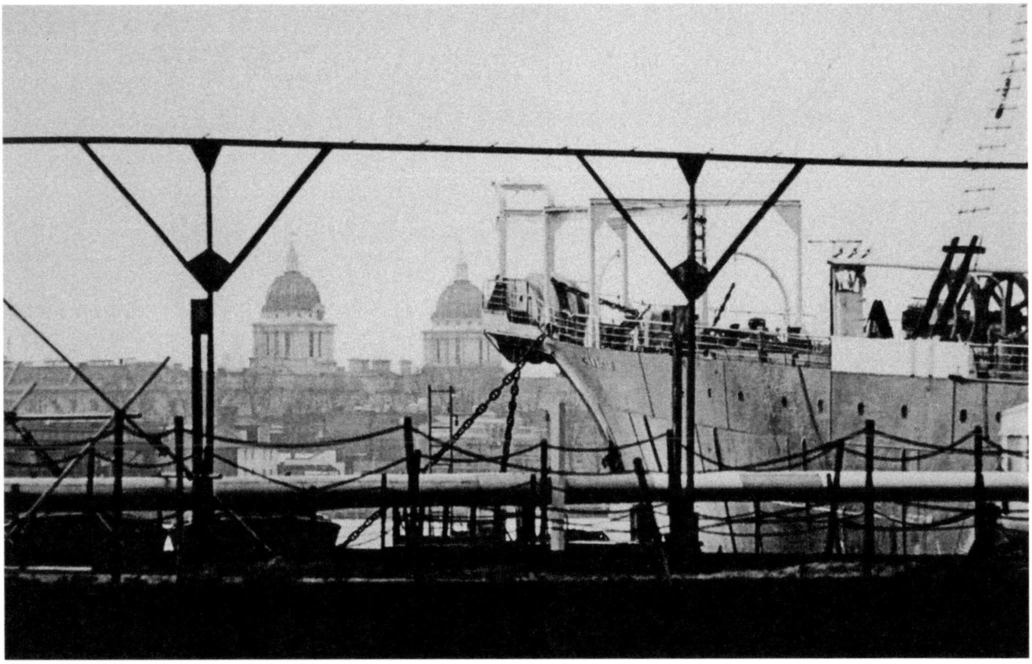

Cable ship *John W. Mackay* was laid up at Enderby Wharf between 1977 to 1990.

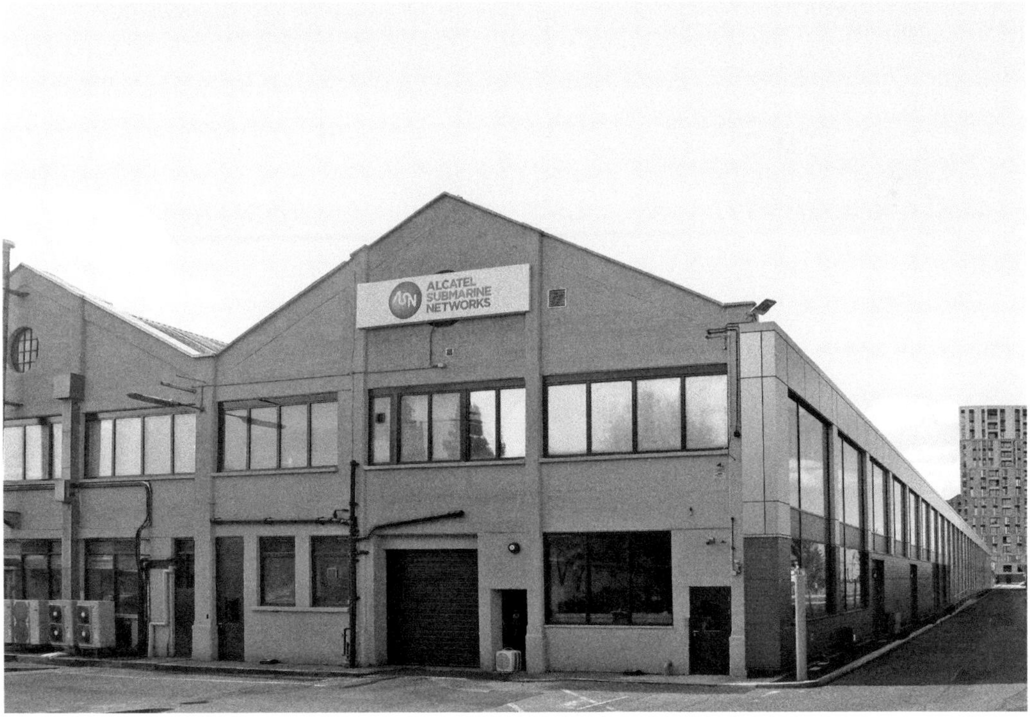


Alcatel Submarine Networks' refurbished factory, Blackwall Lane. The Greenwich-based facility was staffed by an annual average of 180 full-time and part-time employees.

# THE BUILDERS OF BOATS AND SHIPS

Opposite the shipyards at Blackwall, where merchant traders were once built and launched, many Greenwich boatyards were busy building various wooden and iron rivercraft, including fishing boats, lighters, skiffs and sailing barges. The Thames Barge, a hard-working single-mast, flat-bottom boat, used leeboards rather than a keel for stabilisation, allowing the barge to access shallow inlets and tributaries.

## SAILING HAULIERS

Thames Barges were the main river hauliers of many factories, mills and industries, and at one time over 2,000 sailing barges worked the Thames and the coastal waters of Kent and Essex. One of the first barge builders on Greenwich Marsh was Mr Cruden, who constructed his vessels on the foreshore without permission or paying of any rent; subsequently he was forced to cease his activities by an order of the court.

Legitimate barge builders included Shrubsalls, Nortons, Hughans and one of the most famous of all, Pipers. Many of the early sailing barges built at Pipers yard regularly took part in prestigious Thames races, several of their vessels winning prizes.

As sailing barges gradually went out of favour, overtaken by steam-powered tugs able to tow long lines of lighters, many boatyards diversified into constructing other types of rivercraft, a trade which carried on right up until the late 1900s.

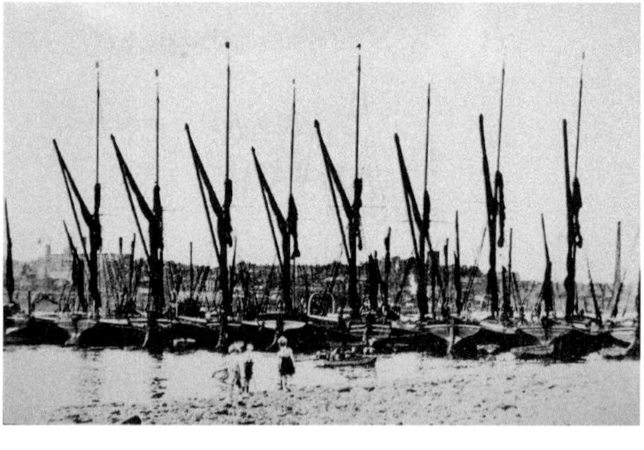

A fleet of Thames barges at Woolwich, *c.* 1905. Mostly used to transport cargo on the Thames and the coastal waters of Kent and Essex, also carrying goods across the channel.

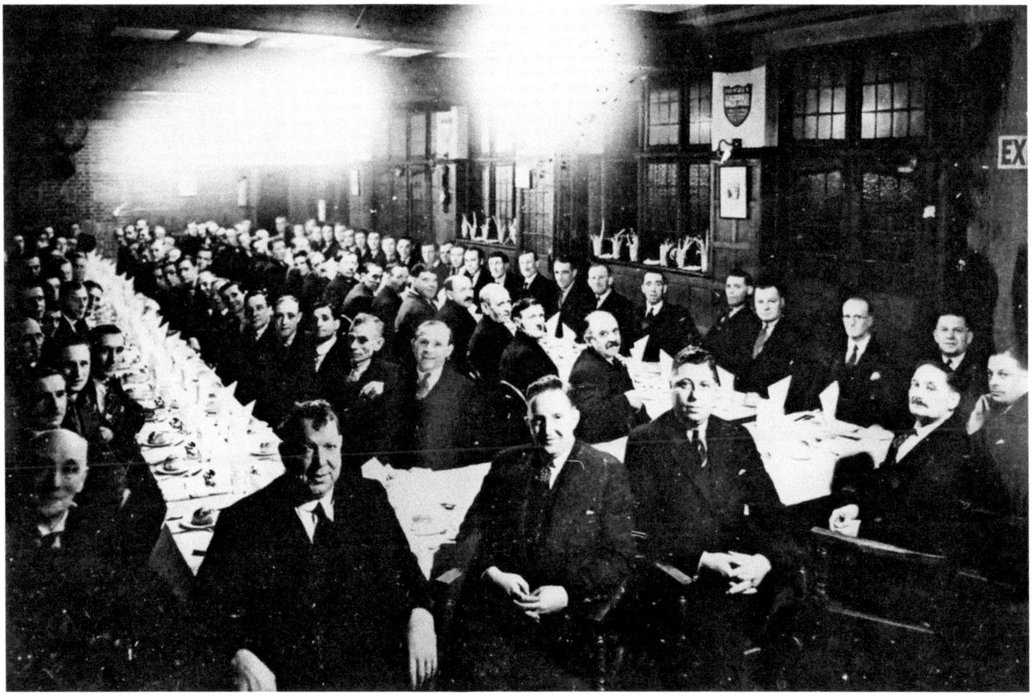


Barge Builders Dinner, *c.* 1933. (Greenwich Heritage Centre)

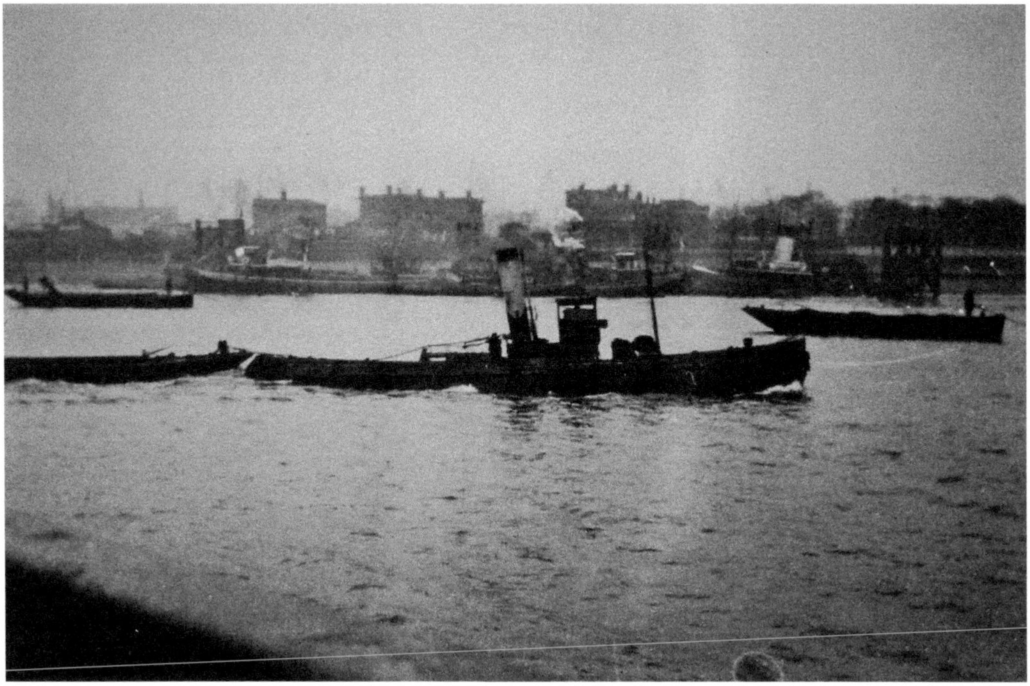

Steam tug towing lighters off Greenwich, *c.* 1934. In the background, lightermen are using the river current and a single oar to manoeuvre their lighters about the river.

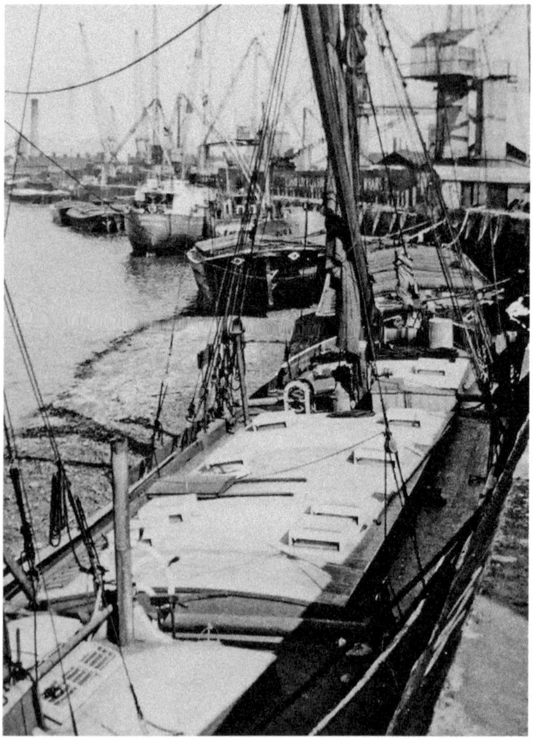

Ballast Quay during the mid-1900s, with various vessels, Thames barges, lighters and coastal ships tied up along the embankment.

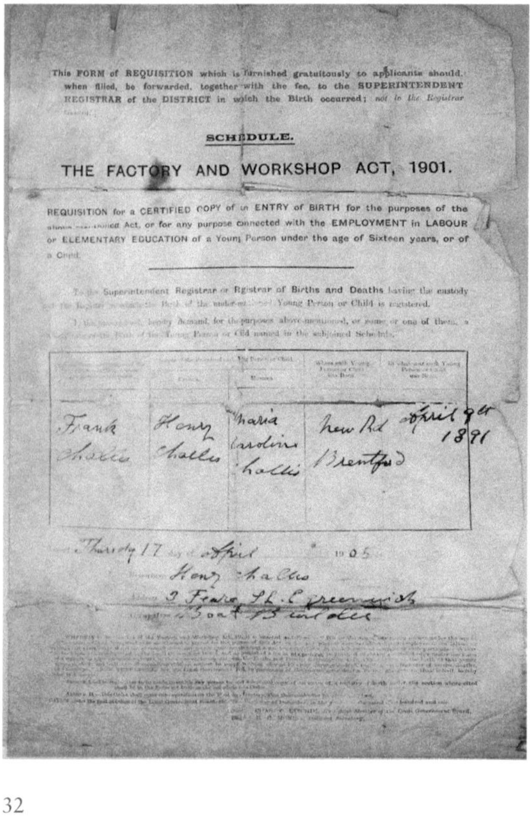

This FORM of REQUISITION which is furnished gratuitously to applicants should, when filled, be forwarded, together with the fee, to the SUPERINTENDENT REGISTRAR of the DISTRICT in which the Birth occurred; not to the Registrar

**SCHEDULE.**

THE FACTORY AND WORKSHOP ACT, 1901.

REQUISITION for a CERTIFIED COPY of an ENTRY of BIRTH for the purposes of the above-mentioned Act, or for any purpose connected with the EMPLOYMENT in LABOUR or ELEMENTARY EDUCATION of a Young Person under the age of Sixteen years, or of a Child.

To the Superintendent Registrar or Registrar of Births and Deaths having the custody of the Register in which the Birth of the under-mentioned Young Person or Child is registered.

I, the undersigned, hereby demand, for the purposes above-mentioned, or some or one of them, a certificate of the Birth of the Young Person or Child named in the subjoined Schedule.

| | | | | |
|---|---|---|---|---|
| Frank Challis | Henry Challis | Maria Caroline Challis | New Rd Brentford | April 9th 1891 |

Thursday 17 day of April 1905

Henry Challis

3 Fears St. E Greenwich

Boat Builder

The Factory and Workshop Act 1901 brought in legislation for the education and working practices of children. It was common for many Greenwich boys to follow in their father's profession as apprentices.

# THE IRON AGE OF SHIPPING

In 1864, a boatbuilder from New York, Nathan Thompson, leased an area of riverside marsh, known as Bay Wharf, from Morden College. The natural bay, formed by a break in the river wall, had been used as a slip for small boat and barge building since the early 1700s. The American boatbuilder designed and developed a production line system for constructing identical rivercraft, cutting down on manpower and manufacturing time, aiming to make iron boats extremely economical to produce.

Thompson's production line boatbuilding system used steam-powered machinery, requiring large financial investments from his company's backers, and for a year the boatyard successfully manufactured iron river boats as predicted. Thompson's, nevertheless, failed to sell all the boats produced and the progressive boatbuilding company soon went out of business.

Marine engineers Maudslay, Sons and Field took over Thompson's boatbuilding site, with the intention of constructing iron-built steamships. The company's origins were in the design, development and production of industrial and marine steam engines, built at its works in Lambeth, South London. After founder Henry Maudslay's death, his sons, Thomas and Joseph, took the family business into shipbuilding and the Bay Wharf yard became an ideal location to build and launch iron steamships.

The first ship, 576-ton steam collier *Lady Derby*, named after Prime Minister John Russell's wife, was launched at the yard in 1865. Even though steam-powered vessels were considered the future of the merchant shipping industry, sail ships continued to hold huge advantages over steamers, which needed to make port during long voyages to take on coal, while sailing ships, powered by the wind, were more economical to operate and required fewer crew to man them.

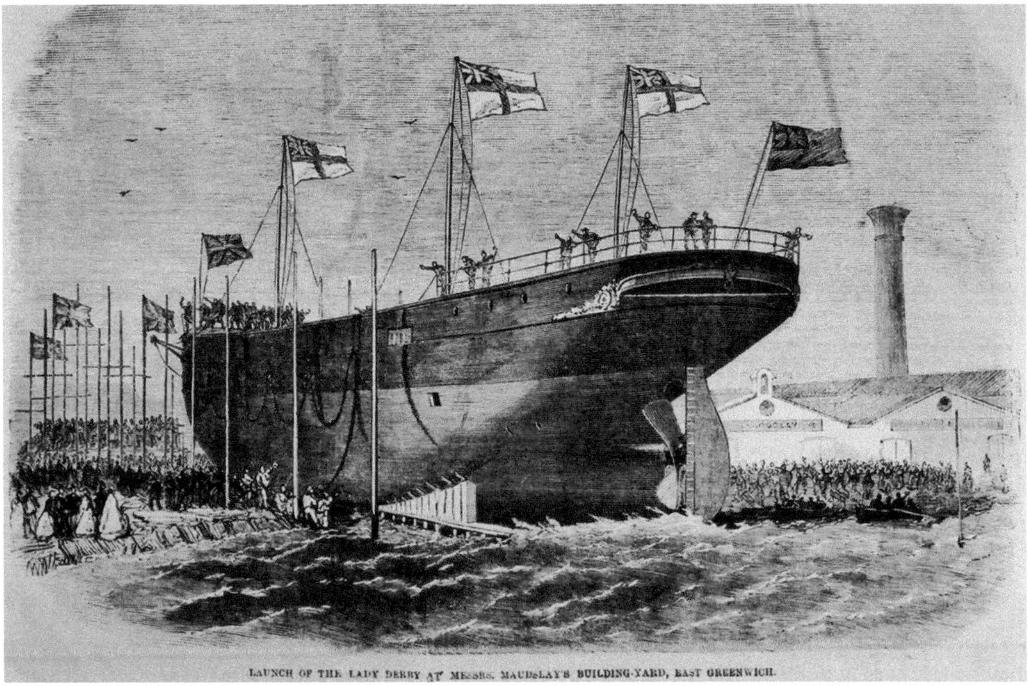


The launch of steamship *Lady Derby* at Maudslay's yard. Ship launches attracted hundreds of enthusiastic onlookers, a popular spectacle for Greenwich workers and residents.

One independent merchant, Scotsman John Willis, owner of the clipper *Cutty Sark*, constructed and launched on the Clyde, commissioned Maudslay's to build two sister ships, the *Blackadder* and *Hallowe'en*. Unlike the *Cutty Sark*, a composite ship, wood clad on an iron frame, both new clippers were built totally in iron. After many profitable, but long and hazardous, voyages, both the *Hallowe'en* and the *Blackadder* were wrecked at sea.

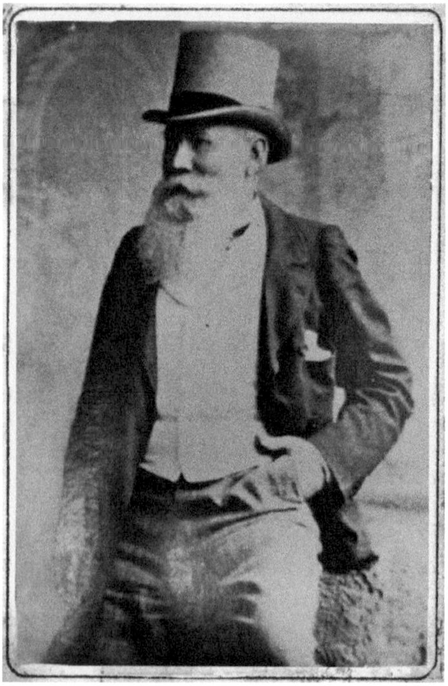

Shipowner and merchant John 'White Hat' Willis, 1817–99.

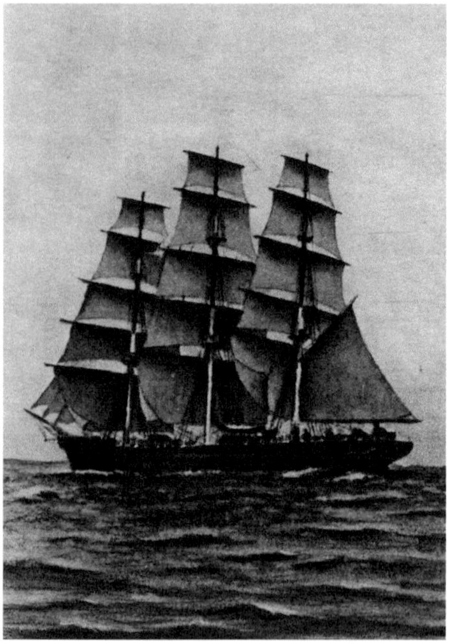

*Cutty Sark* in her prime, late 1800s, now a permanent Greenwich museum ship.

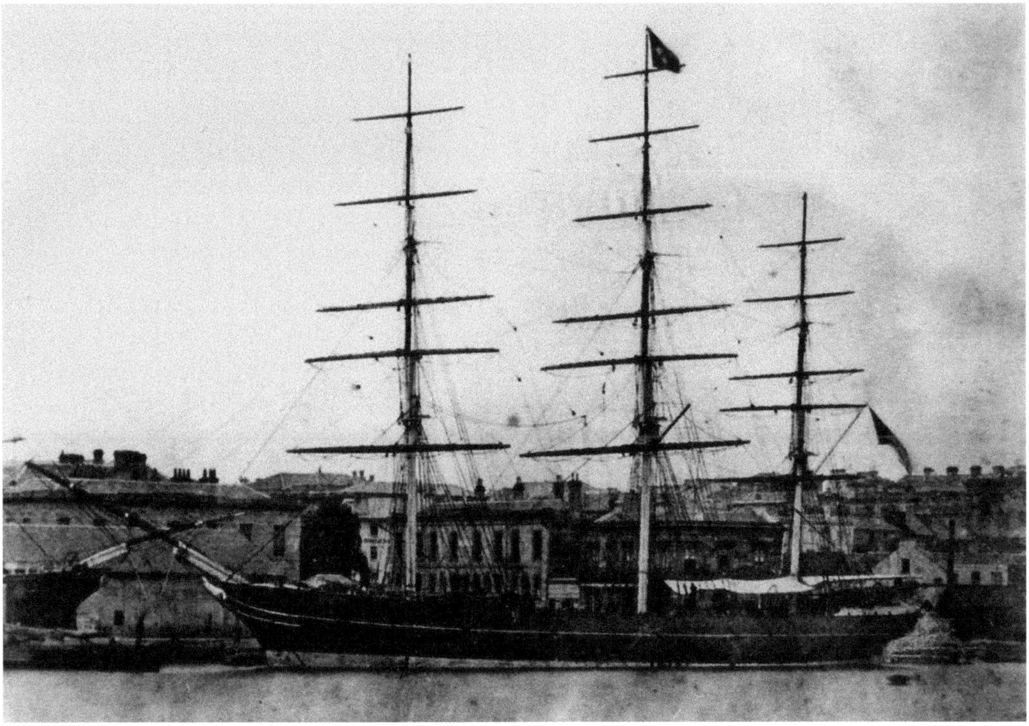

Clipper *Hallowe'en*, launched in June 1870, moored at the quayside during a tea run to China.

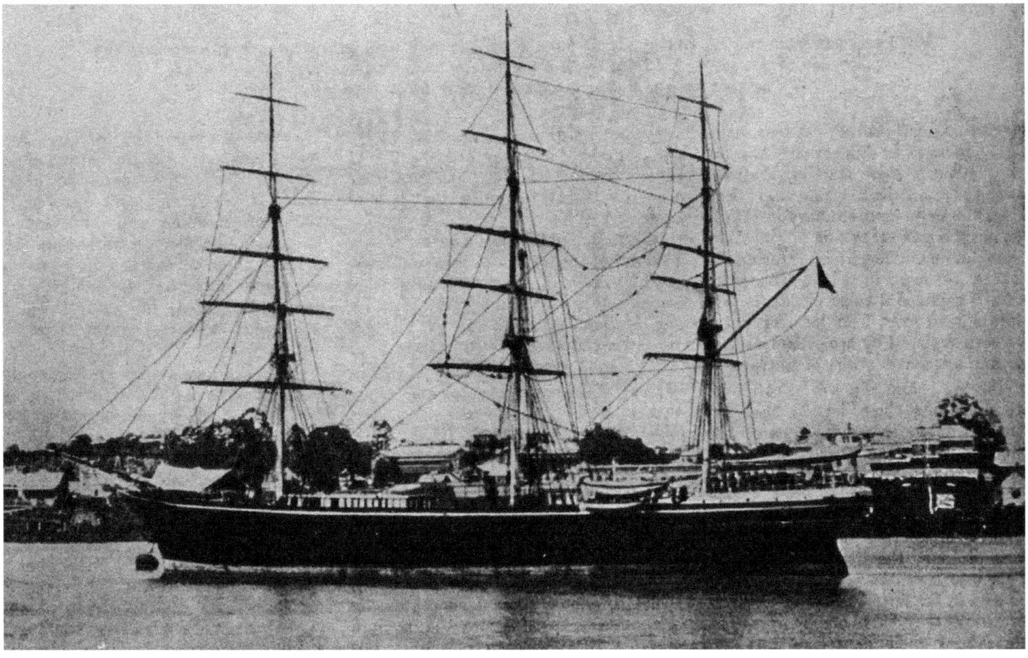

The *Blackadder*, launched in February 1870, almost came to grief during its first voyage to the Cape of Good Hope.

# COMMERCIALISM, MANUFACTURING AND THE CHANGING LANDSCAPE

Many other commercial businesses evolved upon Greenwich Marsh, making and manufacturing various products and materials. In the early 1800s, a works was established for making vitriol, a form of sulphuric acid used in bleaching, and by the mid-1800s a large site was leased to Mowlem, a road contractor, for dealing in stone and aggregates.

Manufacturers on Greenwich Marsh included engineering works Beales, building mechanical road vehicles; Henry Bessemer & Co., a steelworks making large guns similar to those produced at the Royal Arsenal, the site later taken over by Fredrick Walton, inventor of inlaid linoleum; Delta Metal Bronze & Brass Foundry; and Tunnel Refineries, making glucose syrup, the works situated close to Blackwall Tunnel.

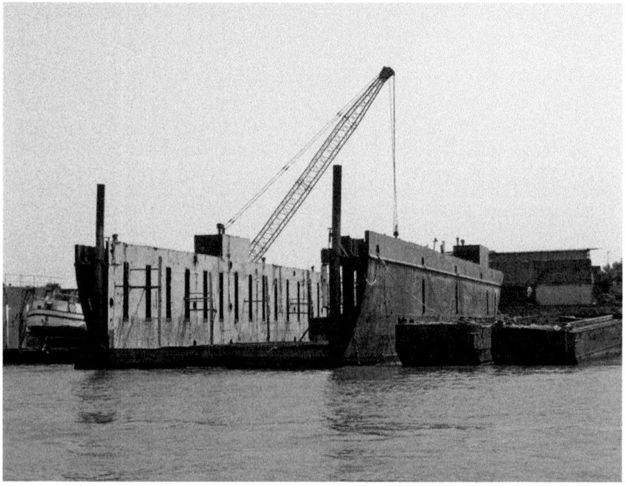

*Left*: Bay Wharf, former site of Maudslay's shipbuilding yard, now occupied by Thames Dry Docking Services, specialists in vessel maintenance and marine support.

*Below*: Blackwall Tunnel southern entrance. On completion the tunnel was opened during Queen Victoria's Silver Jubilee.

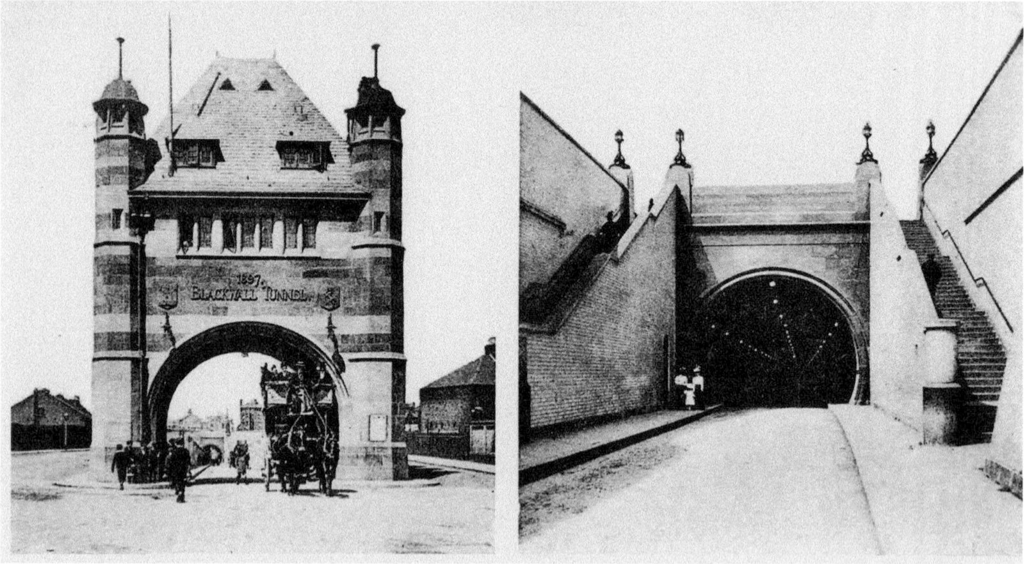

Blackwall Tunnel, which opened in 1897, was built specifically for horse-drawn wagons, pedestrians and cyclists to travel below the Thames between Greenwich's industrial centre on the marsh, and the commercial district of East London. Although the tunnel's construction brought employment to hundreds of workers, many Greenwich Marsh residents were forced to leave their homes, the houses demolished to allow the work to proceed.

Towards the end of the twentieth century Greenwich Marsh, a landscape once crowded with industrial buildings, boatyards, refineries and chemical, cement and aggregate works, had become a neglected wasteland after many of its long-established companies and businesses closed down. With the Greenwich Meridian passing close to the north-west part of the marsh, the site was selected for building an innovative and ultramodern exhibition centre, the Millennium Dome, in readiness to celebrate the approaching twenty-first century.

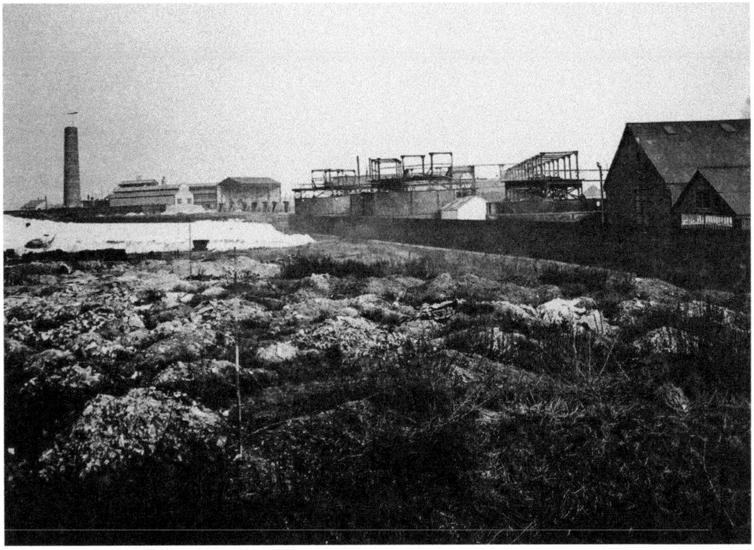

Greenwich Marsh during the late 1900s, a period when industry on the marsh was coming to an end. (Greenwich Heritage Centre)

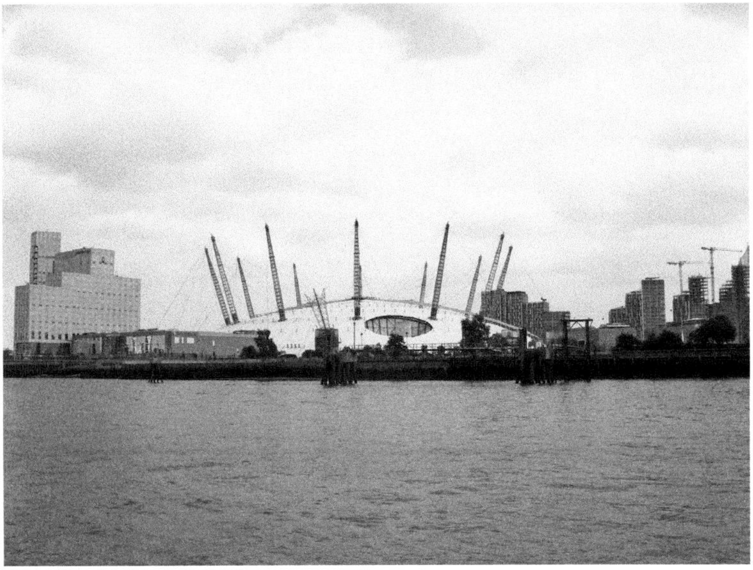

The Millennium Dome, early 2000s, which became known as the O2 Arena.

Architect Richard Rogers' futuristic design incorporated various references to the passage of time. Measuring 365 metres in diameter, the figure corresponded to the number of days days in the year. The white dome canopy was supported by a network of high-tension cables attached to twelve yellow tubular metal struts, each one representing hours on a clock face and the months in a year. Although around £780 million was spent on the project and exhibition within, the venture was a financial failure as attendances fell well below the numbers expected.

Branded a great white elephant, estimated to be costing £1 million a month to maintain, in 2005 the Dome was transformed into a financially successful state-of-the-art concert, sport and exhibition centre, providing employment for hundreds of workers in a lucrative deal with the European telecommunications company O2. After the Millennium celebrations, a regeneration plan set out to make Greenwich Marsh, rebranded Greenwich Peninsula, the centre of an emerging modern East Greenwich business and community district.

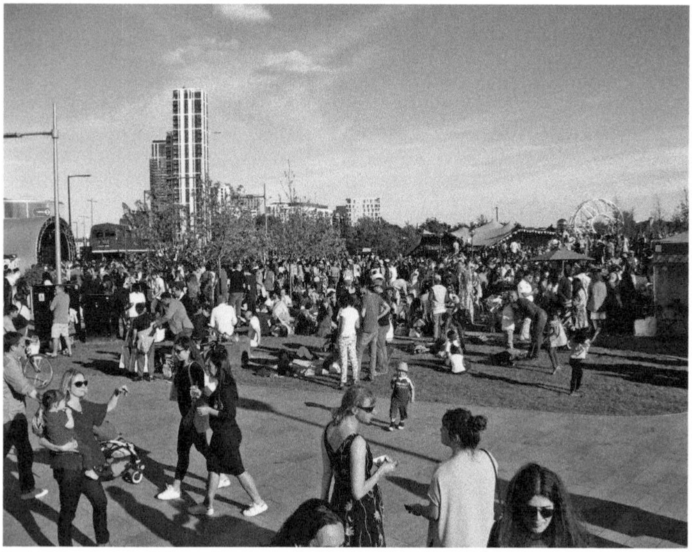

A rejuvenated Greenwich Marsh where the local community enjoy one of many annual festivals.

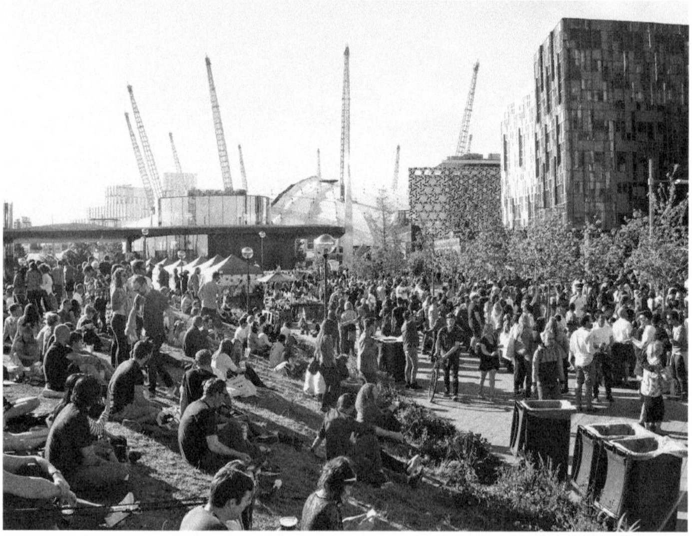

Peninsula life: a new neighbourhood for a new generation of East Greenwich workers and residents.

# WAR AND TRADE

One of the largest employers located in the borough of Greenwich were the royal dockyards at Woolwich and Deptford, Woolwich-based military establishments and Royal Arsenal armaments works.

Not only were these institutions manned by military personal; they all employed civilian workers, essential to the successfulness of Britain's military strength and trading exploits around the globe.

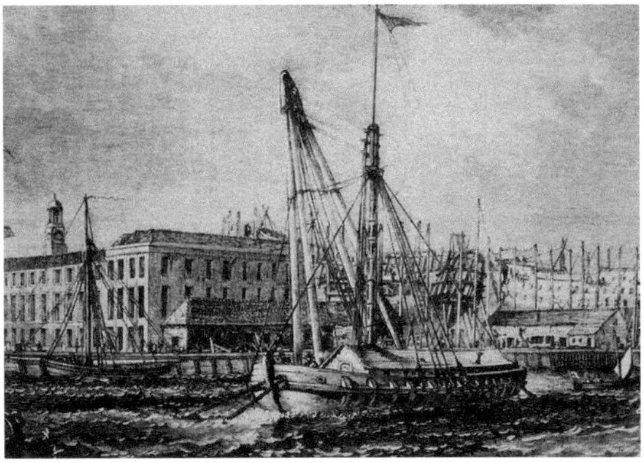

Henry VIII storehouse, Deptford Royal Dockyard. Later enclosed by eighteenth-century building additions, although surviving Second World War bombing, the storehouse was demolished when the site was sold for redevelopment.

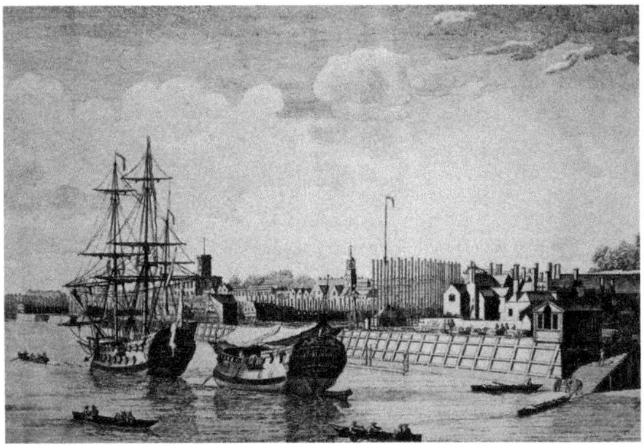

Woolwich Royal Dockyard, mid-1700s. Over seventy vessels were built and launched from the yard including the *Great Harry*, *Sovereign of the Seas* and the *Beagle*.

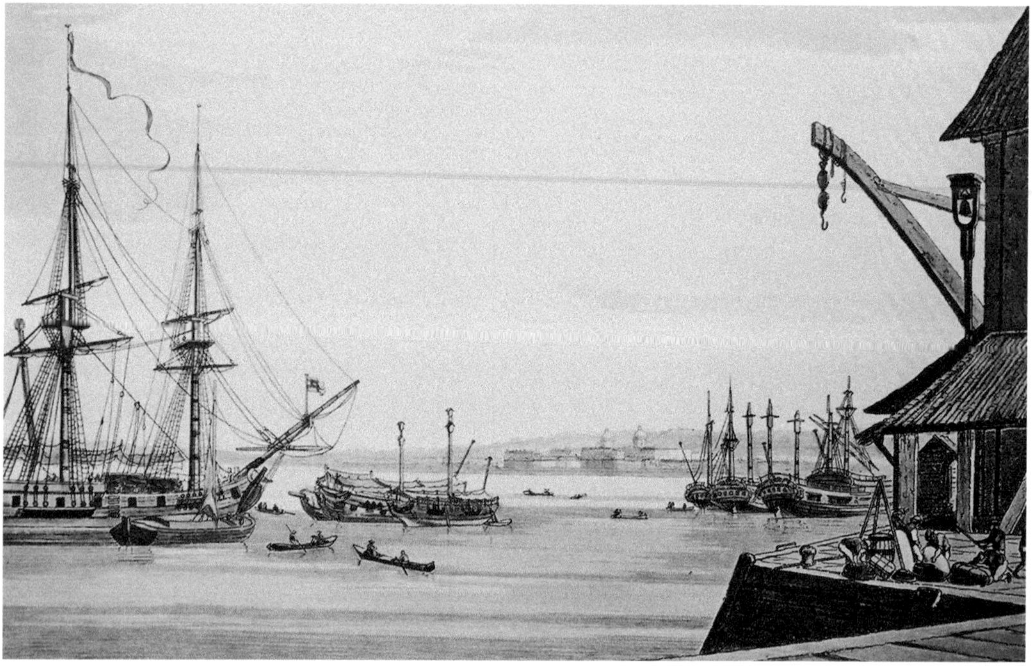

Shipping moored off Deptford Shipyard, where many merchant vessels built at the yard sailed on lucrative trade voyages around the globe, which, for over 200 years, included the trading of slaves.

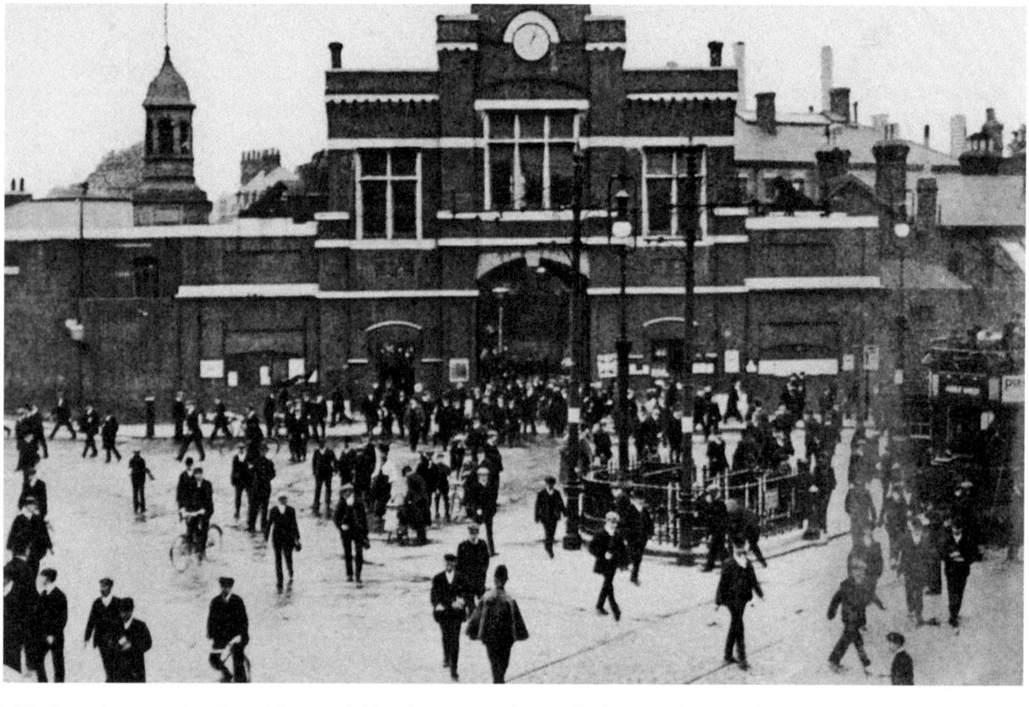

Workers leaving the Royal Arsenal Gatehouse at the end of their shift, early twentieth century.

# ROYAL AND MERCHANT SHIPYARDS

During the reign of Henry VII, the first royal dockyard was established at Portsmouth, on the south coast of England. Most vessels during this period were simply just armed merchant ships fitted out with cannons and crewed by men armed with small arms and bows and arrows.

When Henry VIII came to the thrown his priority was to construct a fleet of warships, the like that no seafaring nation had ever seen, converting his father's repair yard at Deptford into a great royal shipbuilding dockyard. The king then established another Thames side royal dockyard at Woolwich, then just a small wool-trading settlement.

Deptford and Woolwich both grew with the expansion of the dockyards, creating jobs and employment not only for naval personnel and ship crews, but also for hundreds of civilian workers, including carpenters, joiners, painters, blacksmiths, rope and sail makers, and various artisans and craftsmen.

Professional shipwrights employed at the dockyards relocated from all parts of the country, some even migrating from as far away as Italy. Voyages to new lands brought wealth and prosperity to nations capable of building large ship fleets to control the sea lanes around the globe.

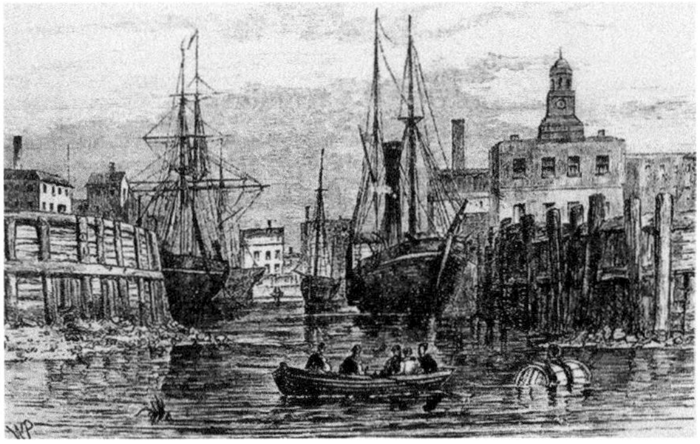

Deptford Creek, *c.* 1810, divided Deptford from Greenwich, the only road crossing by way of Deptford Bridge, on the upper part of the River Ravensbourne.

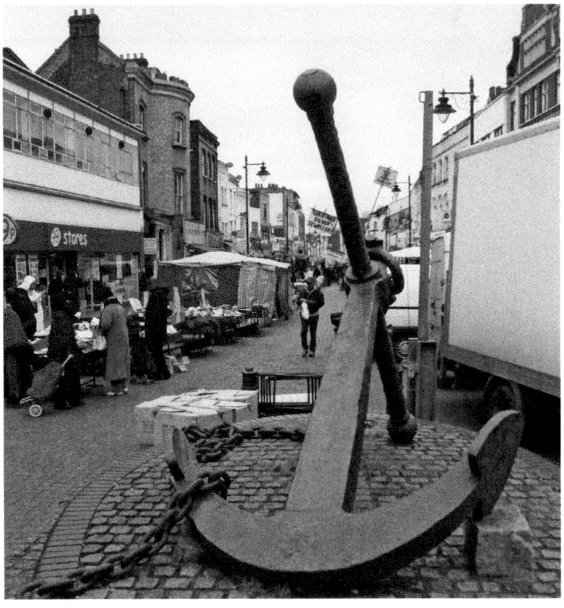


Deptford High Street Anchor, one of the few reminders of Deptford's maritime history, before removal for renovation in 2013.

To enable Britain to become one of those nations and then monopolise world trade, various private shipyards were established adjacent to Deptford Royal Dockyard, for building trading vessels of various design and tonnage, including ships commissioned by the infamous East India Trading Company.

During the 1700s, a large victualling yard was built at Deptford for storing ships' supplies and provisions procured from local merchants and traders, making south London one of the most important mercantile areas in British maritime history, employing an ever-increasing number of workers. Some dockyard workers, however, would go unpaid for their labour, as they were convicts locked away on prison hulks – former warships moored upon the river. Both royal dockyards made use of almost 1,000 convicts a day for manual labour, the bodies of those dying on the job unceremoniously thrown into local marshes.

Many years after the practice of using prisoners as labourers ended, a large quantity of human bones were discovered during building works carried out at the Royal Arsenal site neighbouring Woolwich dockyard, the remains suspected to be those of convicts.

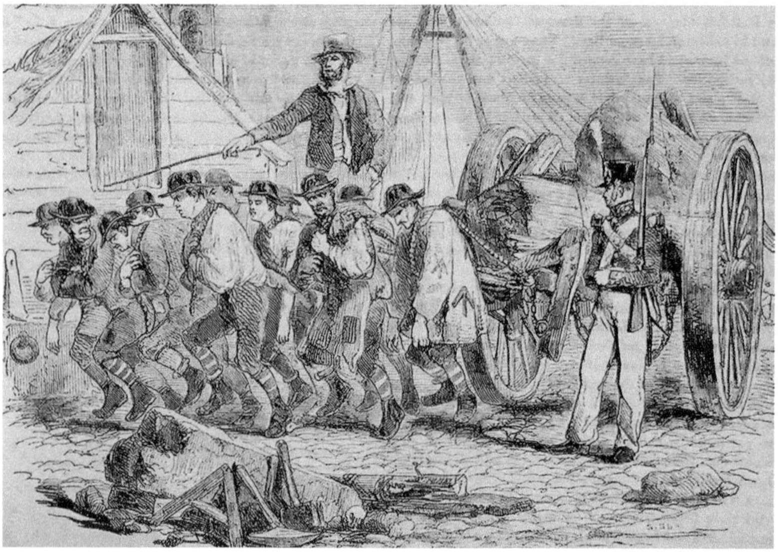

Convicts hard at work labouring at Woolwich Dockyard, c. 1700.

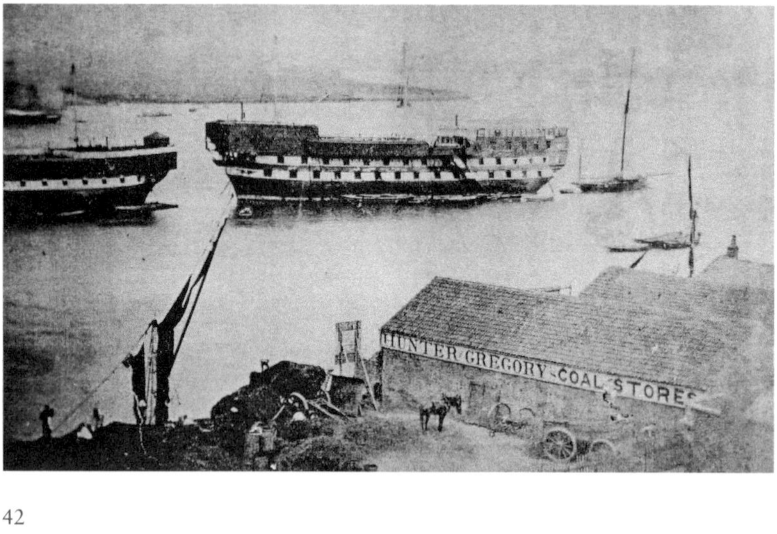


Convict Hulk *Unite*, mid-1800s, moored off Woolwich, where prisoners were held before transportation to penal colonies.

In the late seventeenth century, Peter Czar of Muscovy, or Peter the Great as he was known, rented a house for three months at Deptford, owned by John Evelyn, while studying the latest developments in British shipbuilding, the work of the dockyard shipwrights celebrated throughout the world. The Woolwich Royal Dockyard doubled in size during the early 1700s, as did the workforce, and more ships were launched at Woolwich than from any other English yard.

## FIREPOWER AND ARMED FORCES

After the restoration of the monarchy following the English Civil War, Charles II devised a programme to improve and enlarge the Board of Ordnance works located at the Warren, Woolwich, originally the site of Tower Place, a Tudor mansion, to advance the development and manufacture of armaments, gunpowder and guns. As the Royal Arsenal gradually expanded, the 1,258-acre site included foundries for making cannons, an explosives research laboratory, repository, gun carriage works and ordnance stores.

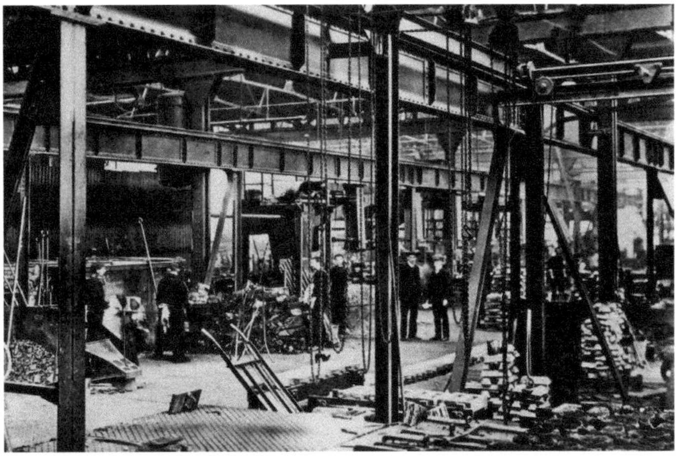

Brass Foundry workshop, Woolwich Arsenal, at the beginning of the First World War.

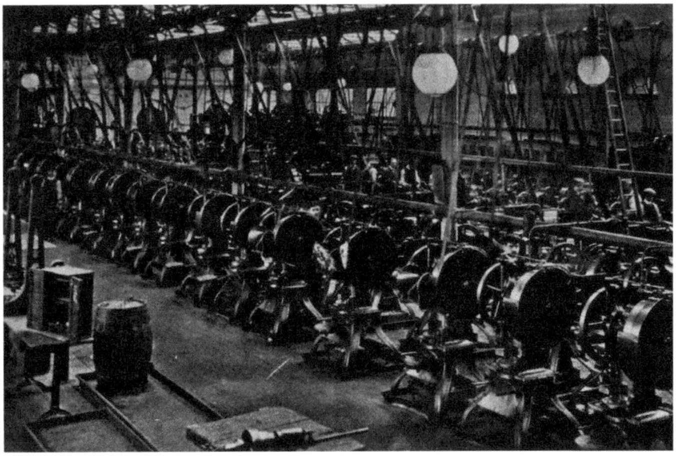

Woolwich Arsenal bullet factory, c. 1914. A total output of small arms bullets amounted to just over one billion seven hundred million during the war.

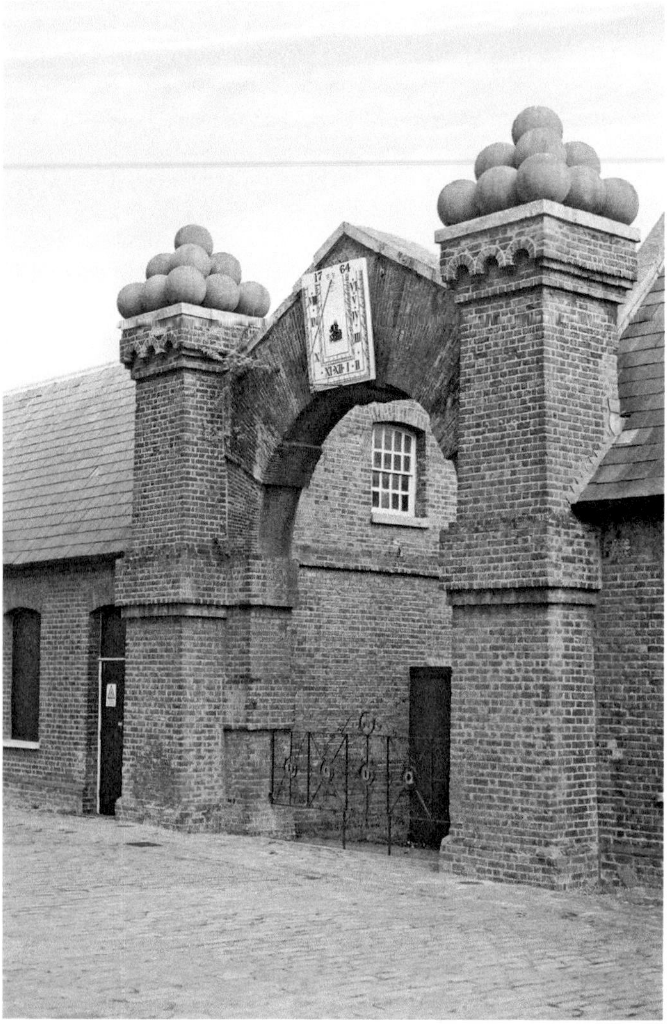

Original entrance, built in 1720, to Dial Square gun barrel works. In 1888, workers formed a football team, Dial Square, a club later to be known as Woolwich Arsenal.

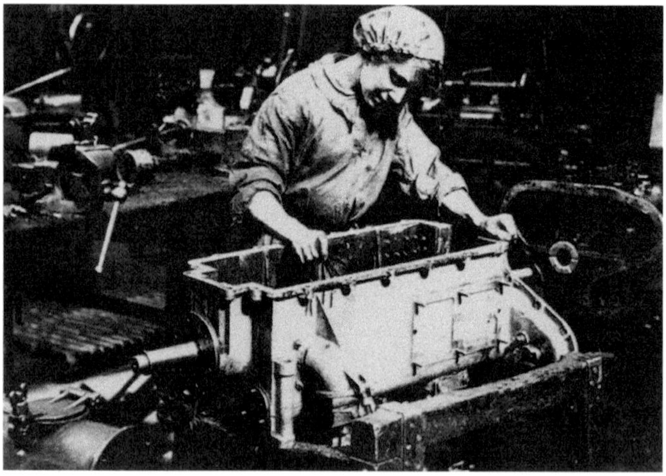

One of the Royal Arsenal's female workers. During the Second World War, 26,000 females, 35 per cent of the workforce, were employed at the armaments site.

Work at the Royal Arsenal created an increase in traffic across the Thames and in 1810 the military began operating their own ferry to transport workers, goods and supplies back and forth. A year later, through an Act of Parliament, permission was granted to allow a commercial ferry for civilian use to run from Old Woolwich to North Woolwich. After the introduction of a ferry service. Two foot tunnels were also built to allow workers to cross the river free of charge, one at Greenwich, opened in 1902, and the second at Woolwich, which opened ten years later.

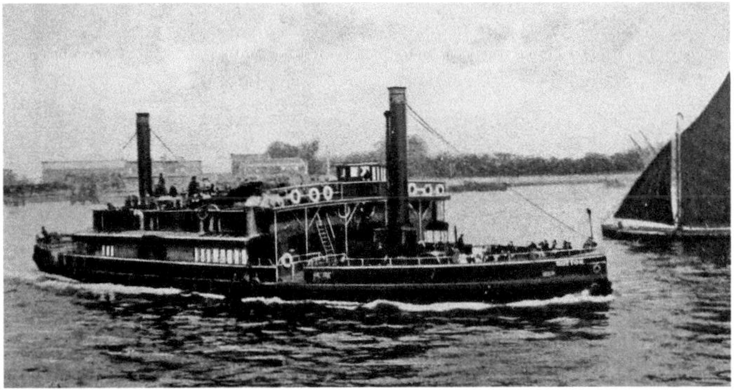

Paddle steamer *Hutton*, c. 1889, named after Woolwich Academy professor of mathematics Charles Hutton. This was one of three Woolwich ferries transporting passengers and traffic across the river.

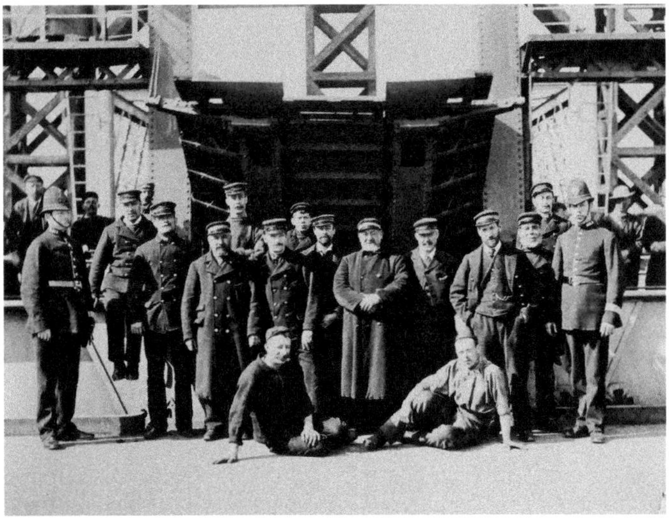

Woolwich ferry crew members, early 1900s. The skipper is at the centre, with deckhands and engineers each side, and stokers at the front. Many early crew members were former Thames watermen.

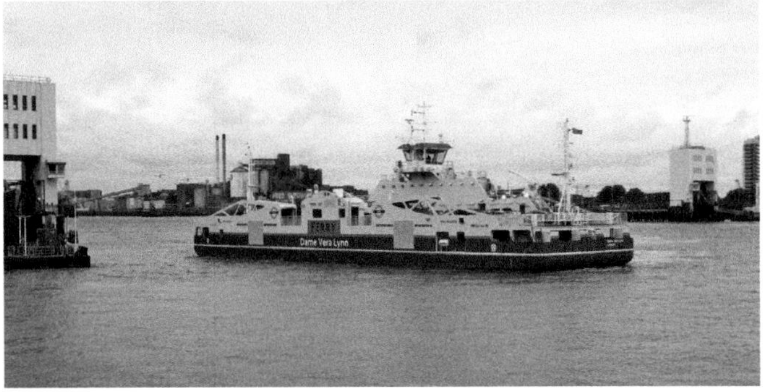

One of the two new Woolwich ferries, *Dame Vera Lynne*, which began operating in 2019.

Within the armaments site, a military academy was founded for training officers and artillery engineers, the academy gaining royal status in 1760, before relocating to Woolwich Common during the nineteenth century. The Royal Artillery Barracks, also once located within the Royal Arsenal, moved to new barracks north of Woolwich Common in the late eighteenth century. The southern frontage, enlarged in the early 1800s, is considered to be the longest continuous architectural structure in Europe.

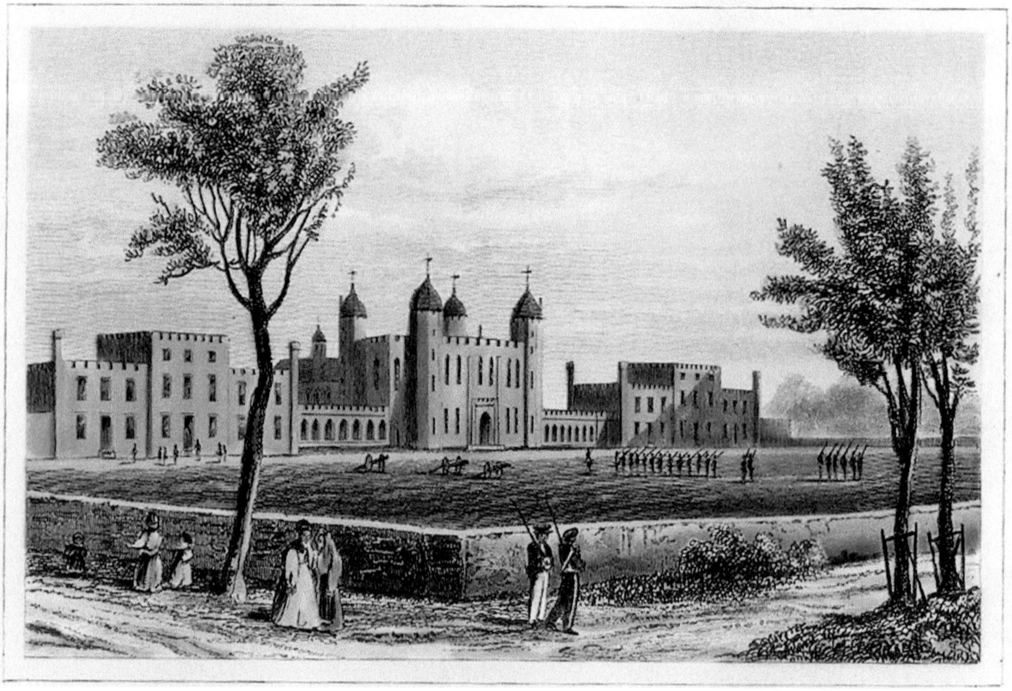

Royal Military Academy, Woolwich Common, where cadets were educated and accommodated in the Tudor-Gothic-style buildings.

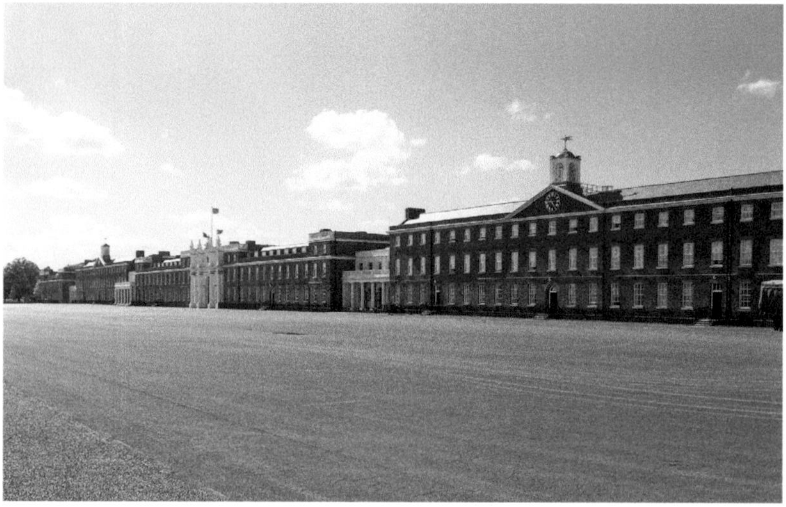

Royal Artillery Barracks, built between 1776 and 1802. Around 400 military personnel once occupied the building.

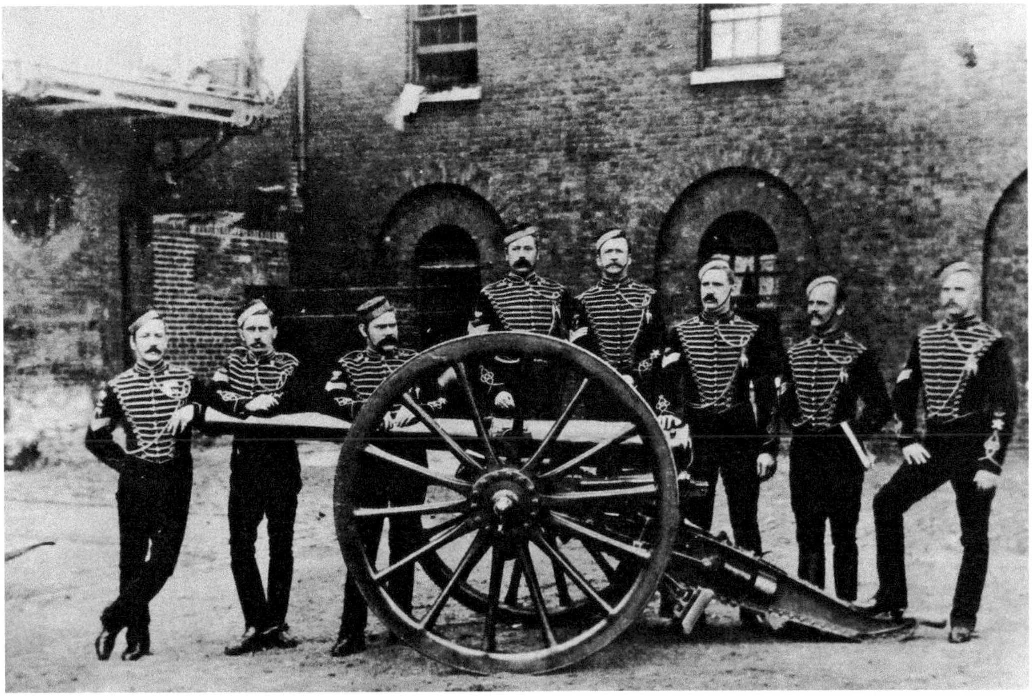

Gun unit of the Royal Regiment of Artillery, originally formed in 1716. By 1780 the regiment comprised of 5,241 officers and men.

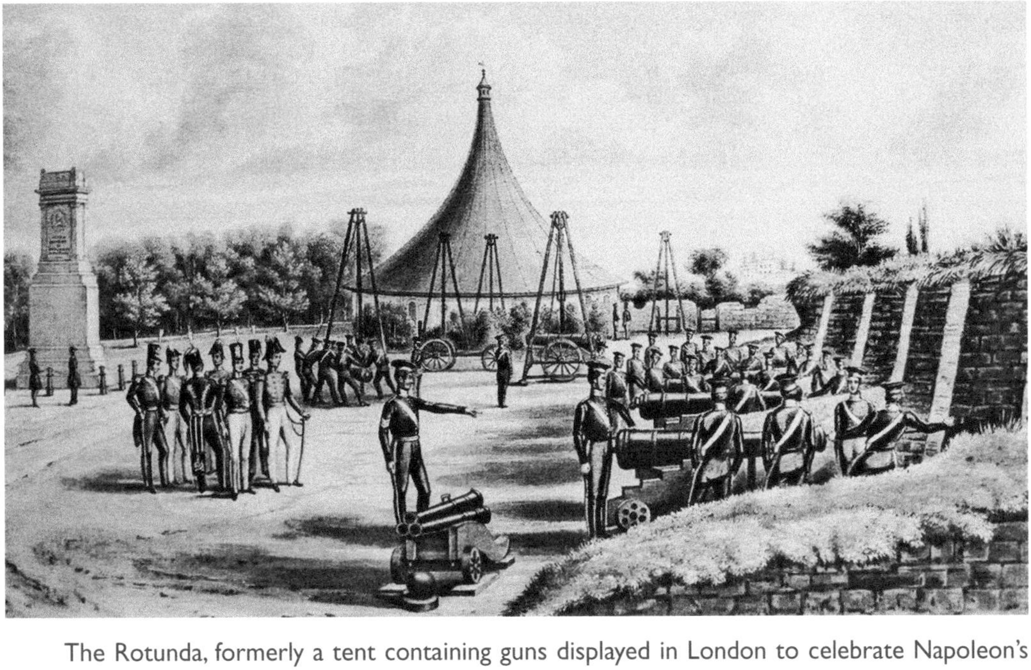

The Rotunda, formerly a tent containing guns displayed in London to celebrate Napoleon's defeat, relocated to Woolwich Barracks in 1816 and converted into a permanent museum in 1920.

# CHANGING FORTUNES

Although working opportunities had resulted in the population of Woolwich increasing from 17,000 in 1821 to almost double this figure by the late 1860s, the need to build larger and more powerful, steel-built, steam-powered vessels eventually brought about the demise of the royal dockyards at Deptford and Woolwich. Due to the silting up of the Thames, it had become increasingly difficult to launch heavy, deep-drafted vessels into the river, and naval shipbuilding at both sites eventually came to an end.

With the closing down of the dockyards, and the Royal Arsenal beginning to lay off workers at the same time, the people of Woolwich fell upon hard times, as many families, dependent on employment in the docks and armaments works, fell into poverty. A benevolent fund was set up to assist them to start a new life overseas, and hundreds of unemployed workers took up the offer to immigrate with their families to Canada.

During the early twentieth century, an increase of hostilities in Europe made it necessary for the Royal Arsenal to employ additional workers to manufacture ammunition and arms for Britain's military forces. In 1915, a government housing scheme created a new residential estate, consisting of 1,200 homes, to house many of these Royal Arsenal workers. First known as Well Hall Estate, the properties were designed to include a variety of building materials and finishes – stone, brick, timber-framing, rendering, and tile and slate hanging – to give the impression of a typical English village.

It was estimated around 80,000 workers were employed at the Royal Arsenal site during the First World War; however, after hostilities ceased, operations were scaled down and the

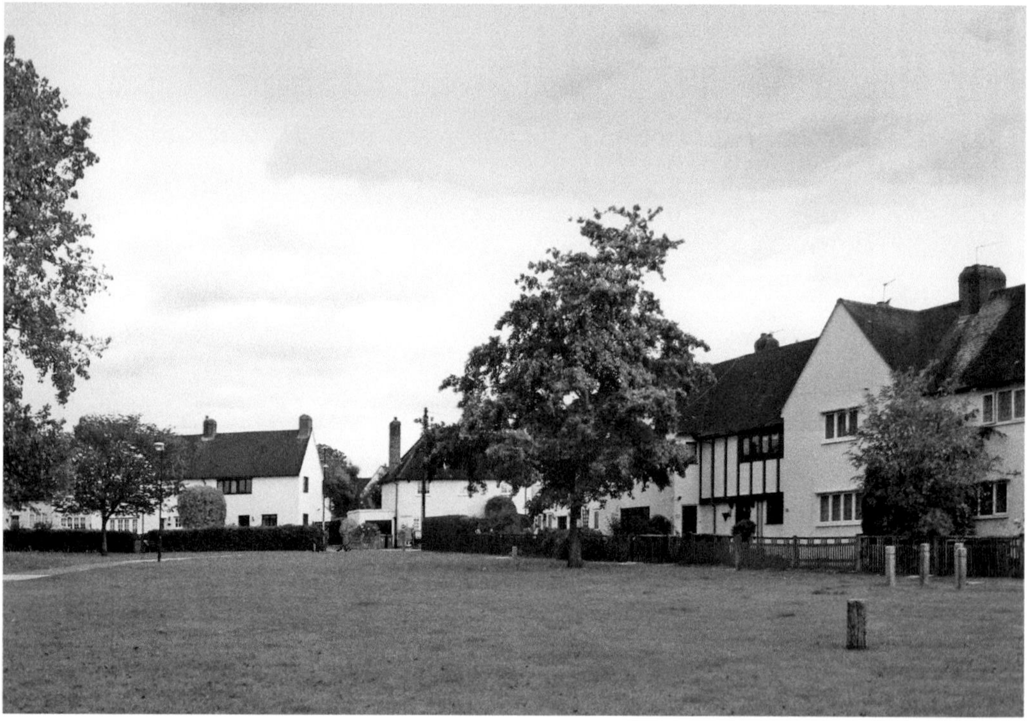

Once homes for armaments workers, the Progress Estate is located within a highly populated suburban area 4 miles from the centre of Greenwich.

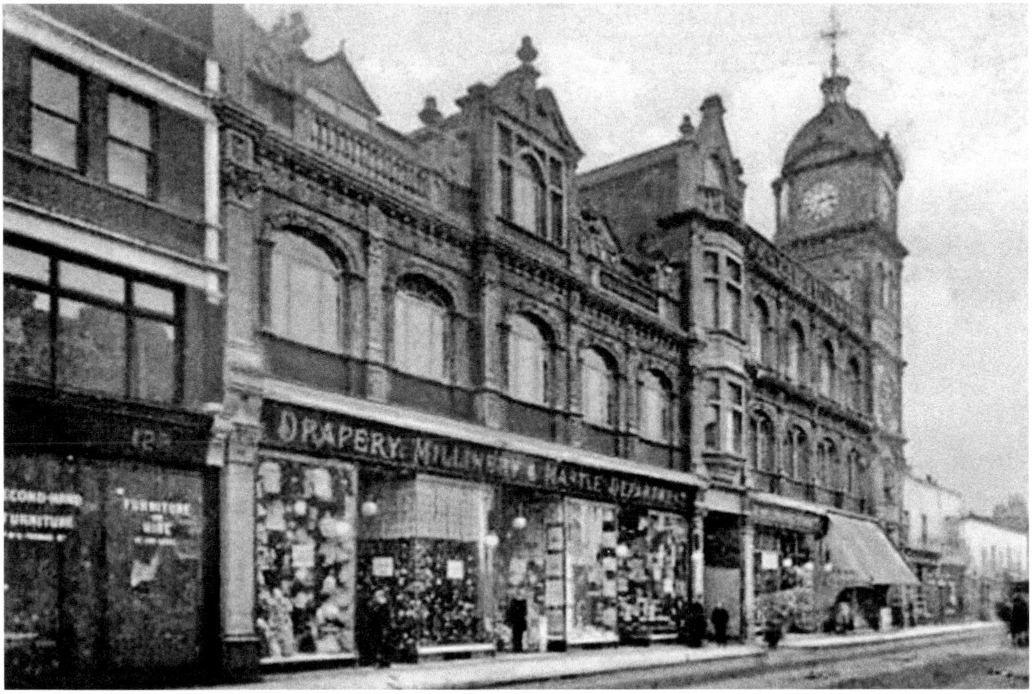


Co-operative central premises and store, Powis Street, Woolwich, *c.* 1900. The store building was later enlarged to the right of the clock tower, matching the store façade to the left.

workforce had halved by the Second World War. Before the outbreak of the war, Well Hall Estate was purchased by Progress Estates, a subsidiary of the Royal Arsenal Co-operative Society, founded by twenty Royal Arsenal workers as a trading store in 1868.

A percentage of the society's early profits accumulated from food retail were utilised to fund education projects, and by the early 1900s, financial ventures moved towards commercial, political and social activities, along with housebuilding and estate management.

By the outbreak of the Second World War, the old dockyard sites were being used for various commercial purposes, including a cattle market at Deptford and stores at Woolwich. After suffering from bomb damage during the Blitz, in the 1960s town planners selected the dockyards as suitable for residential redevelopment.

Following the scaling down of munitions manufacturing after the war's end, areas of the Royal Arsenal became surplus to requirement and were disposed of. The whole site had eventually closed by 1994, destined to become another large housing development project. Many of the principal historic buildings, however, were saved, some refurbished for use as residencies, while others were converted into bars, restaurants, cafés and retail outlets, commercial ventures providing employment for a new workforce.

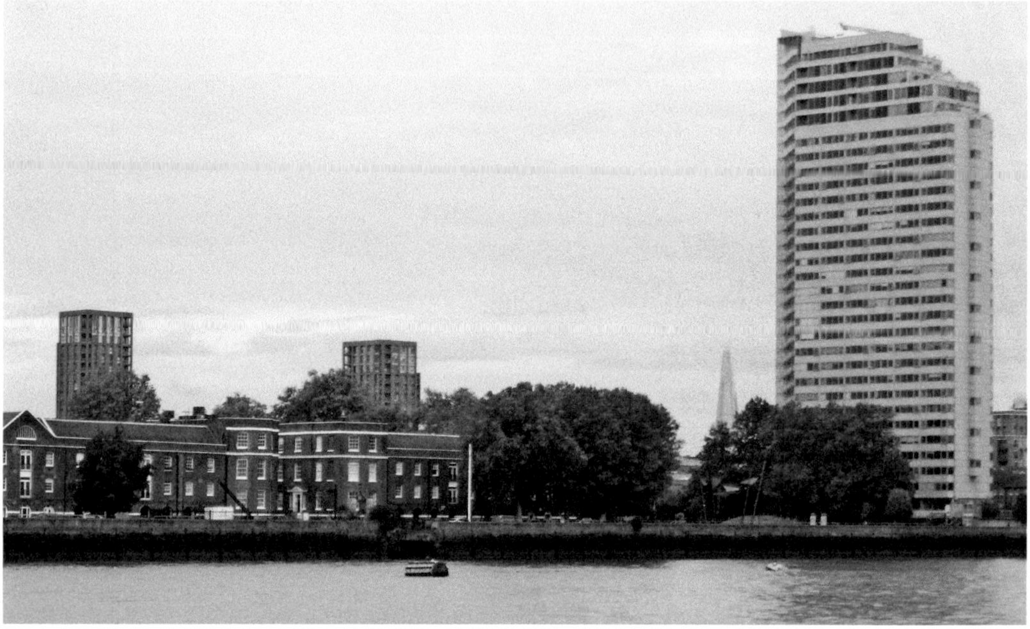

Deptford Dockyard Royal Victualling Yard buildings to the left, refurbished for residential use, with former Pepys Estate block of council flats to the right, renamed Argon Tower after refurbishment and conversion into luxury apartments.

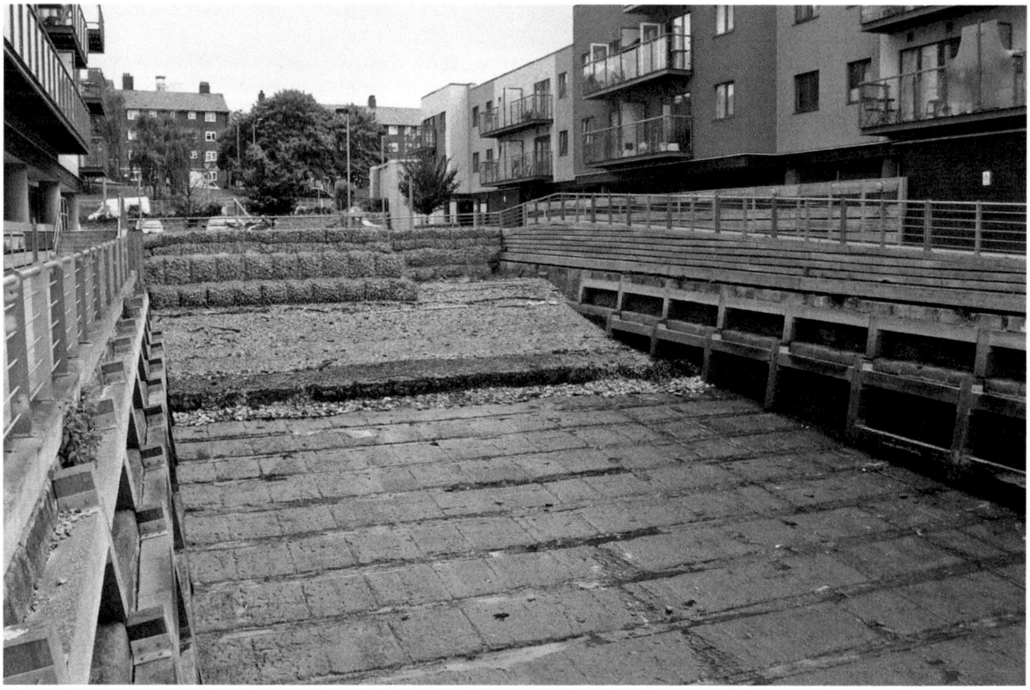

Remains of one of the Royal Dockyard slipways, Woolwich, a majority of the dockyard coming under residential redevelopment during the early 1970s.

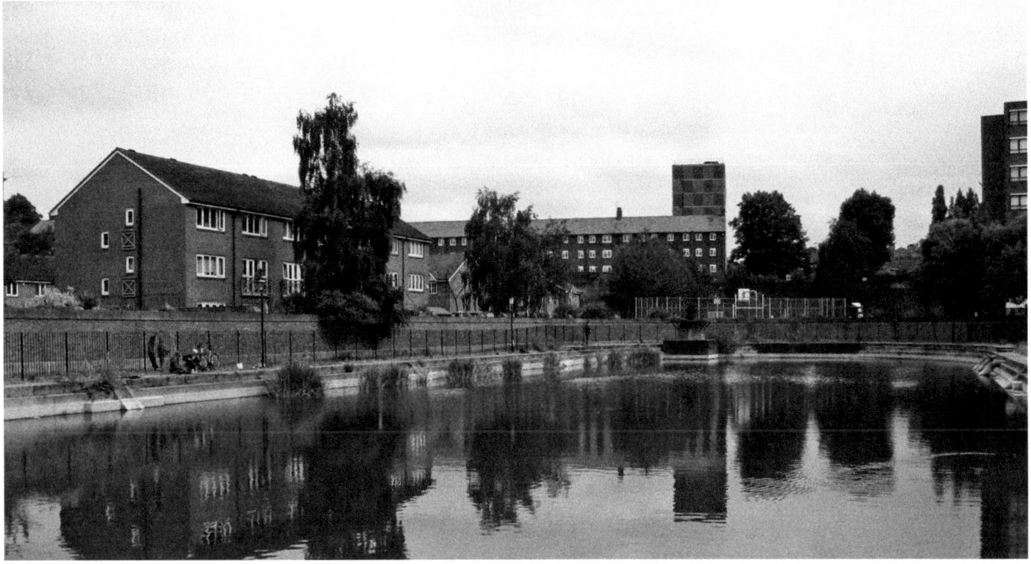

One of the existing Grade II listed dry docks at Woolwich Royal Dockyard, converted into fishing ponds, destined to become a design feature of a proposed riverside residential property development.

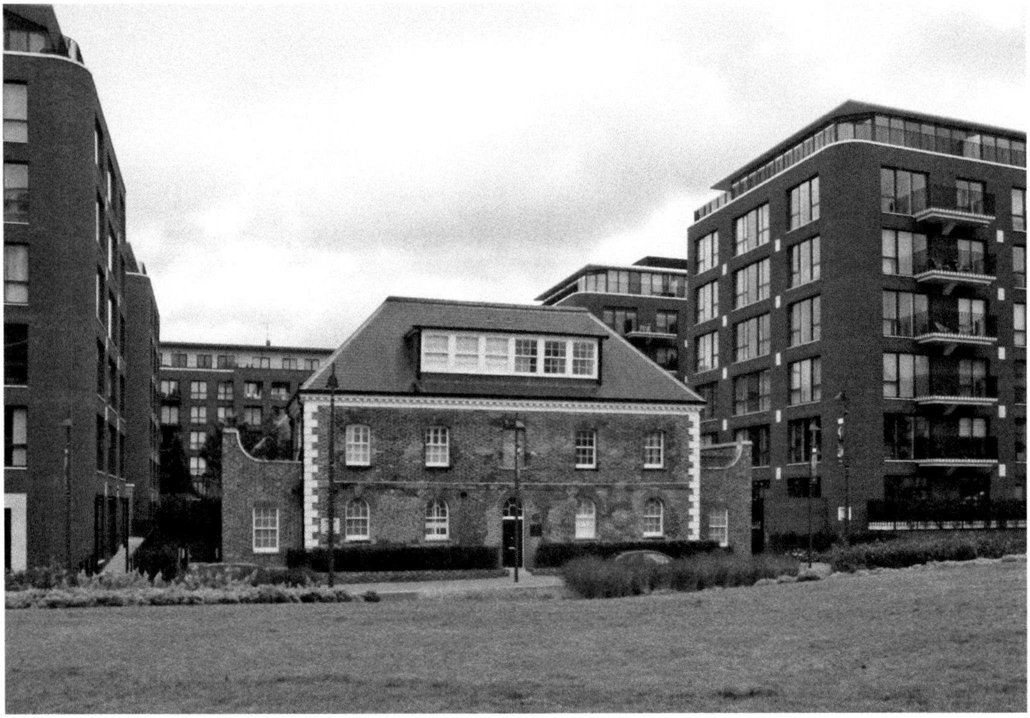

Former Royal Laboratory West Pavilion. The seventeenth-century Grade II listed building is one of a pair, the oldest buildings on site, refurbished as part of the Woolwich Arsenal residential development Pavilion Square.

# WORKING PLACES

One of the earliest working practices carried out at Greenwich was fishing, a time when the riverside settlement was occupied by a community of Anglo-Saxons. These first fishermen used traps to catch fish when the tidal Thames was teaming full of numerous species, including salmon, trout, eels and even sturgeon. There was also a diverse assortment of shellfish such as oysters, muscles, whelks and cockles gathered from the riverbank and estuaries. One of the most popular catches on the Thames as a source of food was the smelt, a small silver fish considered a delicacy.

By the early nineteenth century, fishing had become an important family affair, many fishermen's sons, from the age of nine, following in their father's trade and training for seven years as an apprentice.

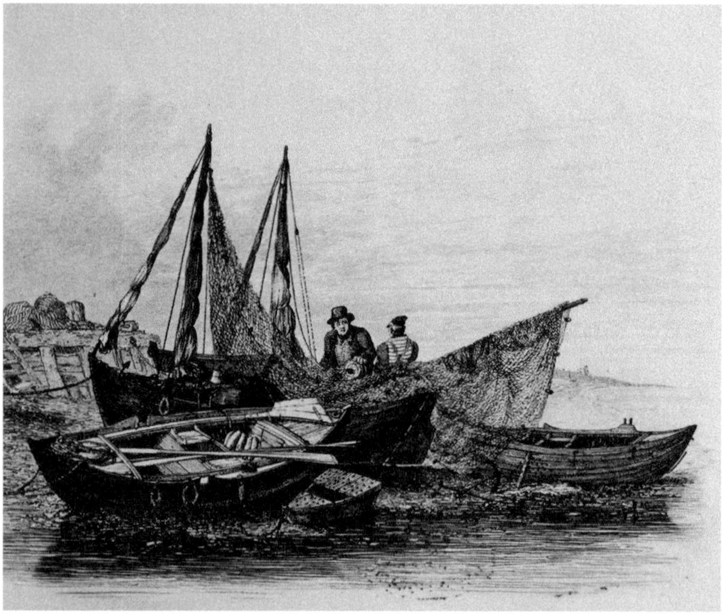

Fishermen and their peterboats on the Greenwich embankment, *c.* 1828.

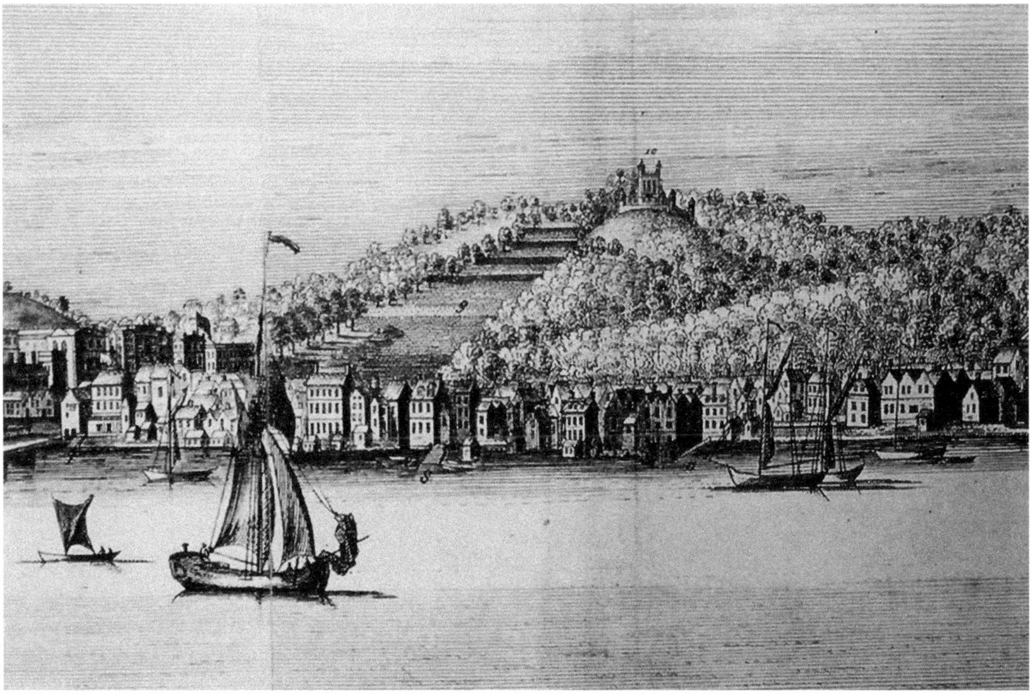

Various small fishing craft off Billingsgate Dock, located to the west of the Royal Hospital.

# FISHERMEN OF GREENWICH

The most versatile Thames fishing vessel was the clinker-built peterboat, many constructed at Greenwich yards, each with a small hold amidships for storing fresh catches of fish. Peterboats varied in size and style depending on what part of the river was fished – above or below London Bridge.

Much of the fish caught from boat or shore would have been sold at a market near Fisher Lane, which ran along the perimeter of Greenwich Hospital, where a fish market had existed since at least the late 1600s. The development of Greenwich Hospital and the surrounding area brought about the market's closure and the destruction of all that remained of medieval Greenwich to make way for a new market selling all types of local produce, situated centrally within a square of elegant buildings.

The Thames at this time was full of young sprat and herring, known as whitebait, and local fishermen found a ready market selling to many riverside inns, such as the Ship Tavern and the Trafalgar Tavern, where members of parliament travelled downriver to dine.

Billingsgate Dock, adjacent to Greenwich Foot Tunnel, was once the base of a North Sea fishing fleet with a history going back to the fourteenth century. Smacks from Greenwich were sailing north well into the mid-1800s, a very dangerous but profitable trade. The Greenwich-based fishing fleet relocated to Grimsby soon after it became more economical, and faster, to transport fish to London from the north-east fishing ports by goods train, the boats sailing back from the fishing grounds of the North Sea taking much longer to deliver their catch.

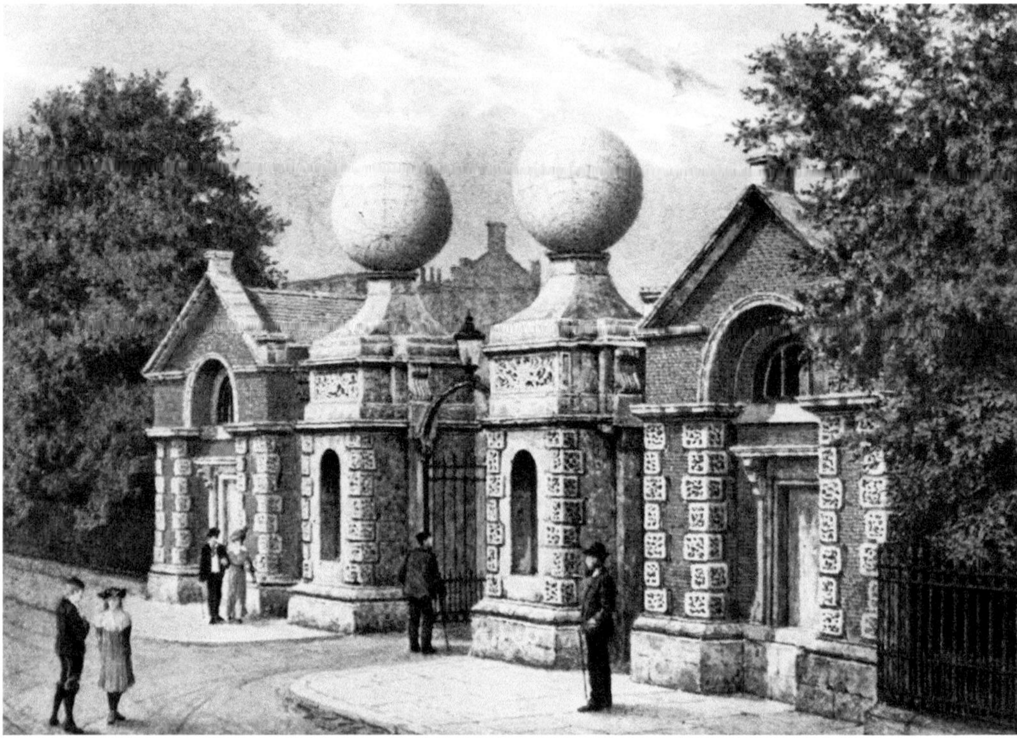

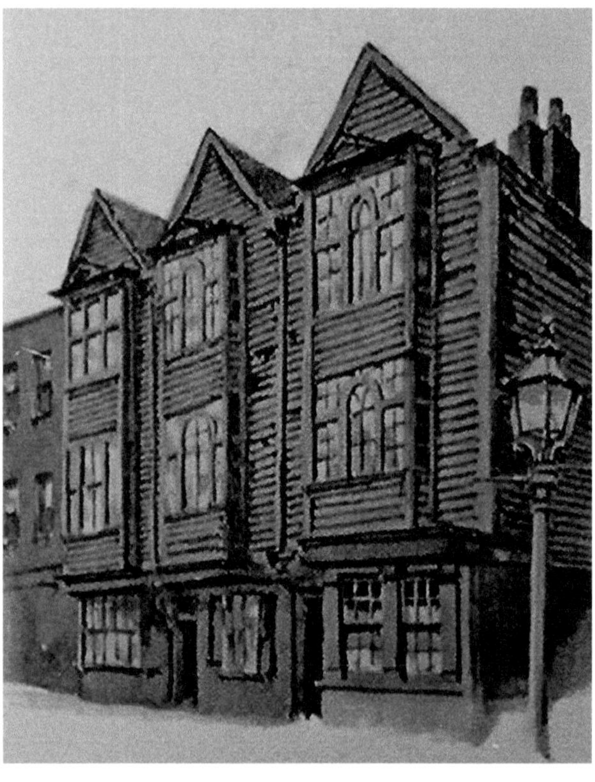

*Above*: Royal Naval College West Gate, dating from 1752, was moved from its original position and re-erected on the former market site during the mid-1800s.

*Left*: Medieval Greenwich buildings close to Billingsgate Dock, demolished in the 1830s, during improvements made to the town centre.

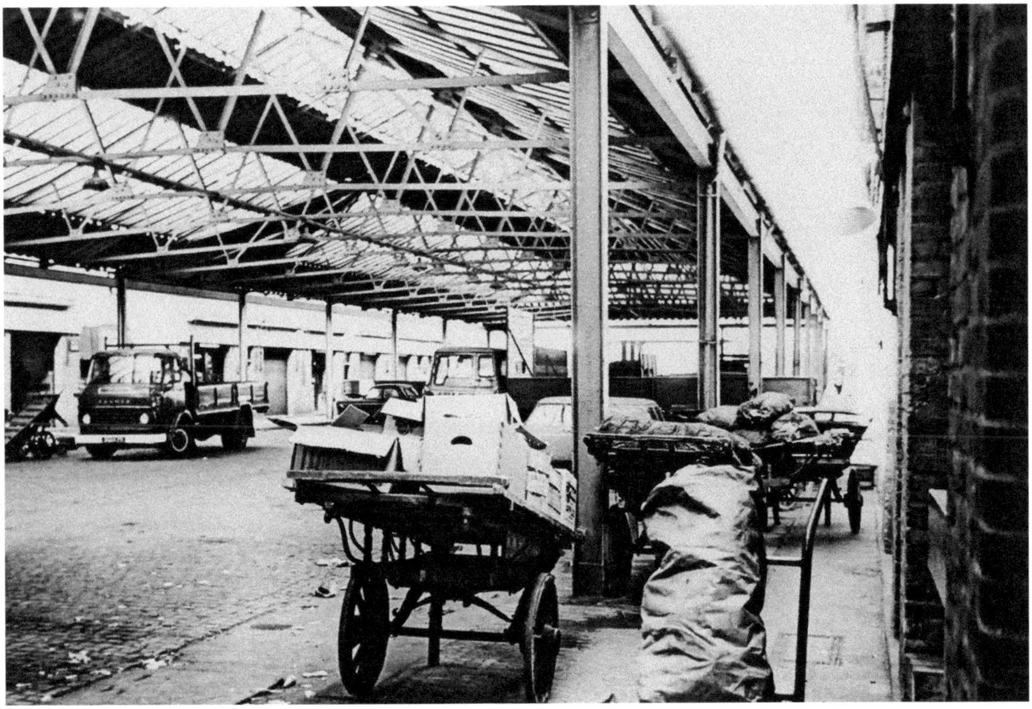

*Above*: Covered market square, mid-1900s, at the end of a day's trading.

*Right*: Market entrance off College Approach, today a vibrant arts, crafts and food market.

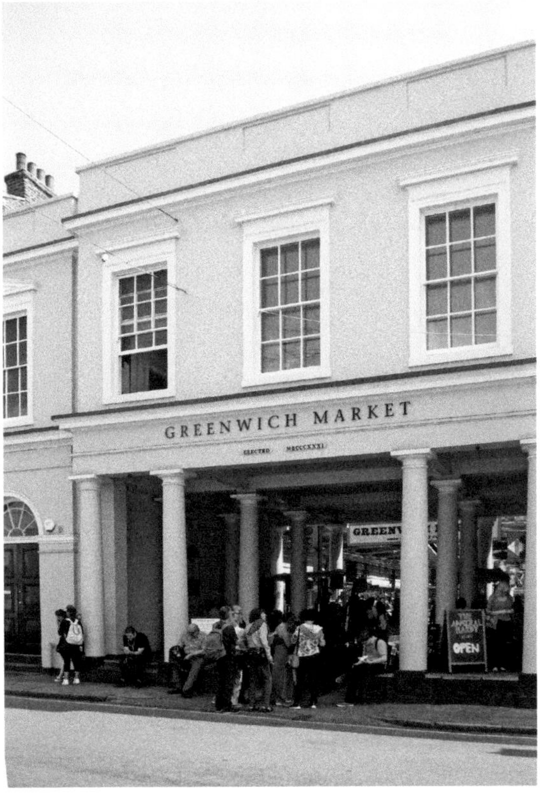

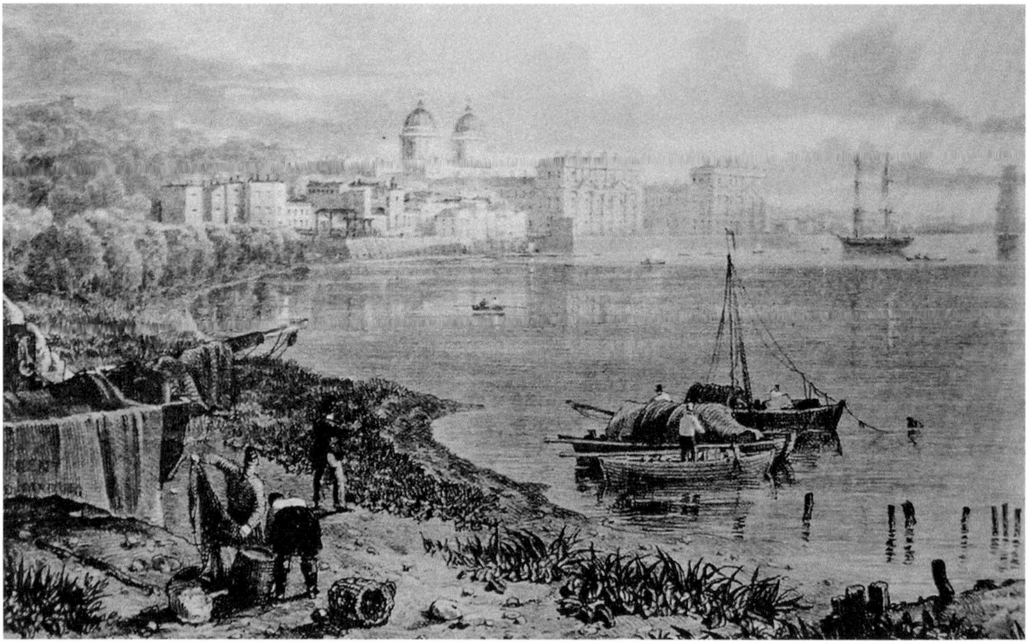

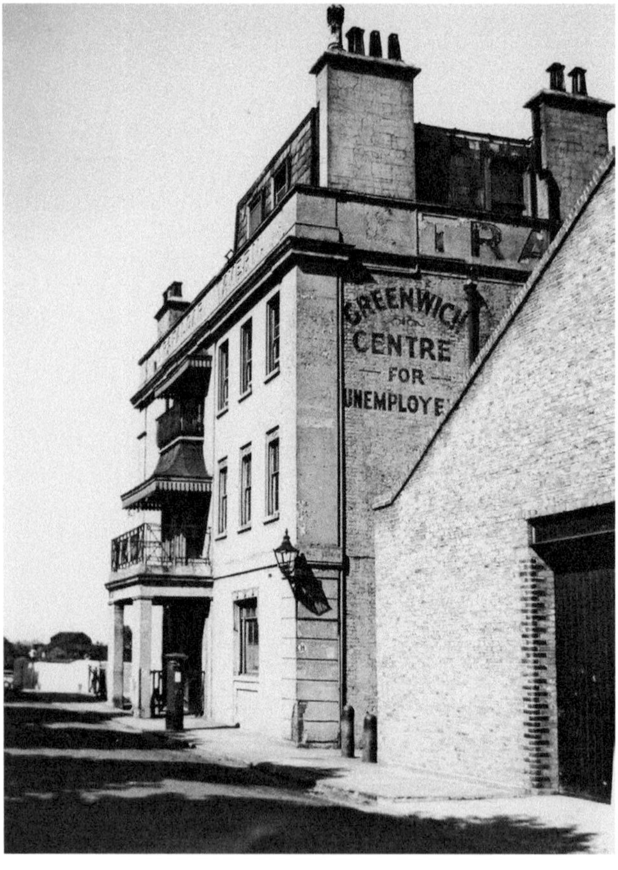


*Above*: Fishermen east of the Royal Hospital hanging out nets to dry on the embankment, when the Thames was once teaming with all species of fish, *c*. 1800.

*Left*: The Trafalgar Tavern, Park Row, favoured dining place for Liberal MPs during the mid-1800s.

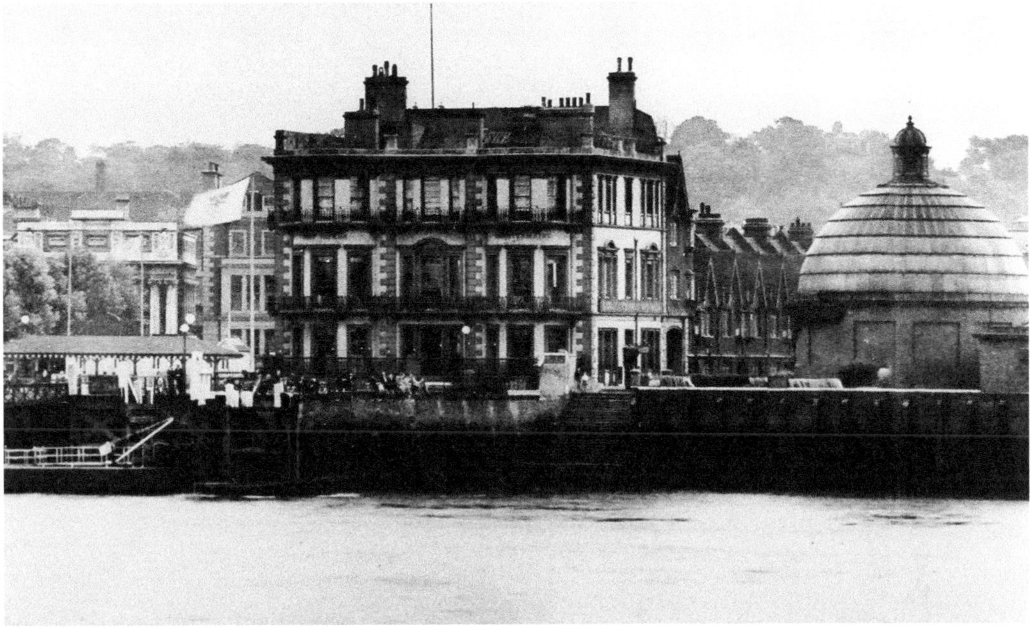

The Conservatives preferred the Ship Tavern, one of the largest Greenwich inns at the time. The tavern was demolished after suffering bomb damage during the Second World War. (Greenwich Heritage Centre)

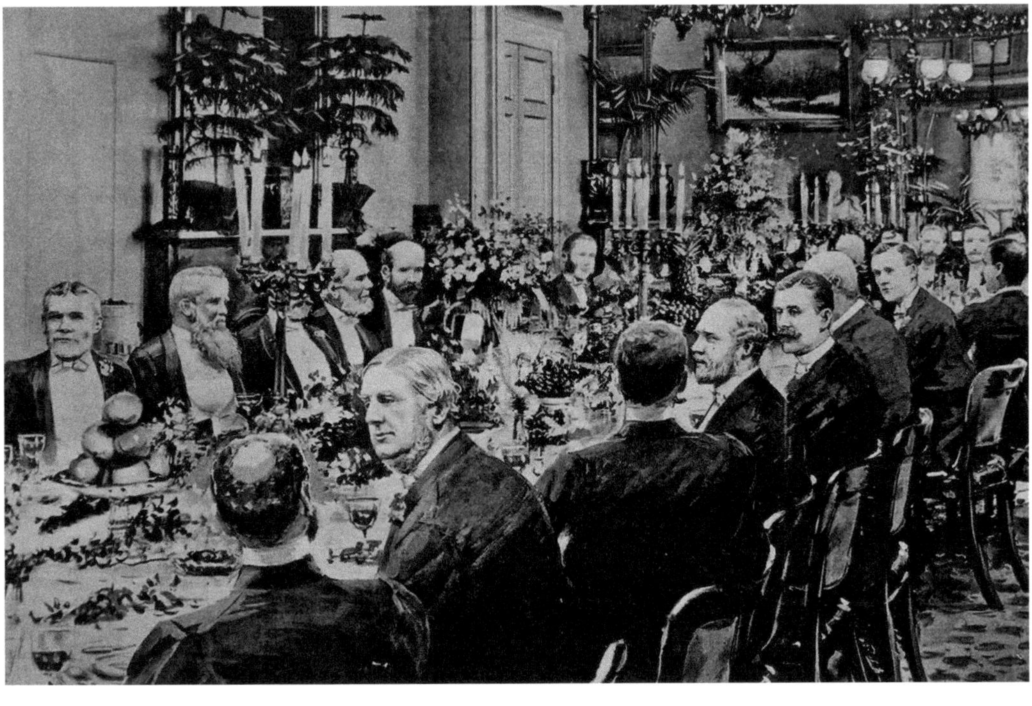

Members of Parliament dining out on whitebait at Greenwich, a tradition that began in the early 1800s during parliamentary recess.

# BREWING HEALTHY BEER

Fish dinners were often washed down with a flagon of ale, and another early trade carried out in Greenwich was brewing. The first recorded brewers were the Flemish monks who founded a monastery, which included a brewhouse, at Greenwich after the manor was gifted to the Abbey of St Peter at Ghent by Princess Elstrudis, daughter of King Alfred.

At this time beer was brewed in the Flemish tradition, using hops rather than brewing conventional unhopped Saxon ale.

By the reign of Henry VII, hops were more commonly used in English brewing, although both hopped and unhoped beer continued to be produced for many centuries. Beer was relatively free from bacteria, the antiseptic properties of alcohol killing off life-threatening microorganisms, which made the beverage much safer to drink than water. Brewing in Greenwich carried on throughout the Tudor and Elizabethan periods, and well into the late 1800s.

Because of the overconsumption of gin during the late eighteenth and early nineteenth centuries, drunkenness was said to have caused an increase in crime and deprivation. The 1830 Beerhouse Act was passed to liberalise regulations for brewing beer. The intension was to encourage beer drinking as an alternative to drinking gin, the legislation increasing the number of Greenwich breweries and brewhouses. The Greenwich brewing trade also brought a rise in working opportunities for various associated local industries – cooperages, maltings, bottle making and milling.

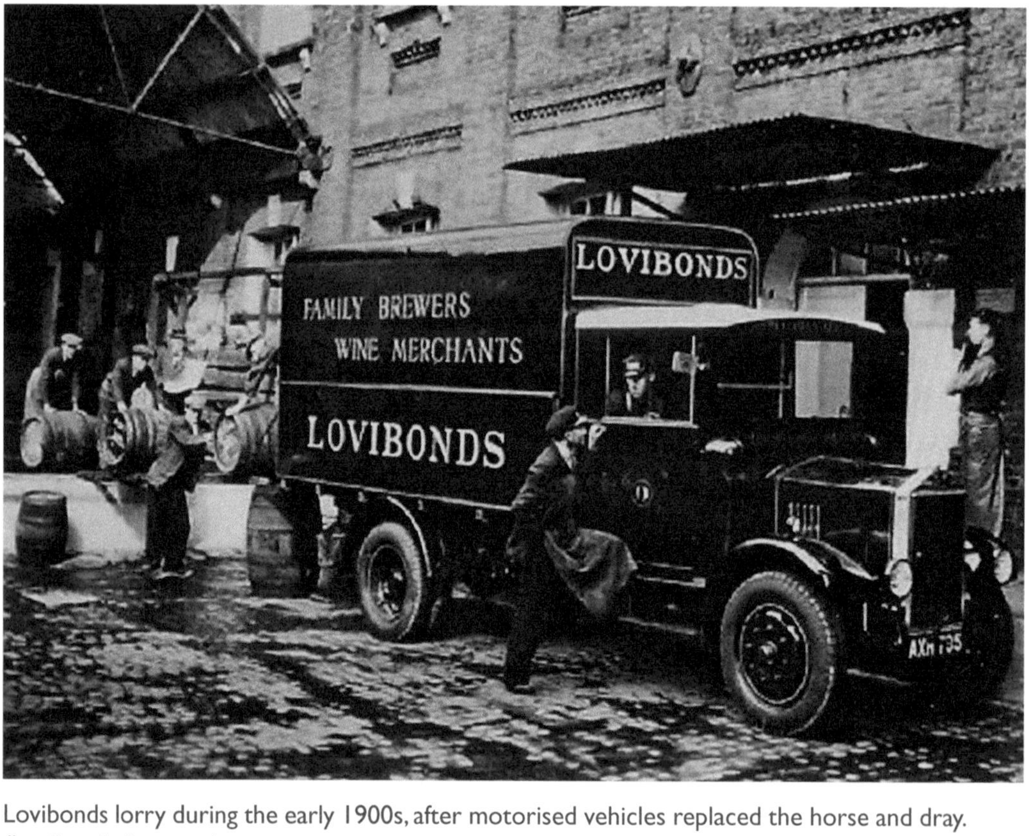


Lovibonds lorry during the early 1900s, after motorised vehicles replaced the horse and dray. (Lovibonds Brewery)

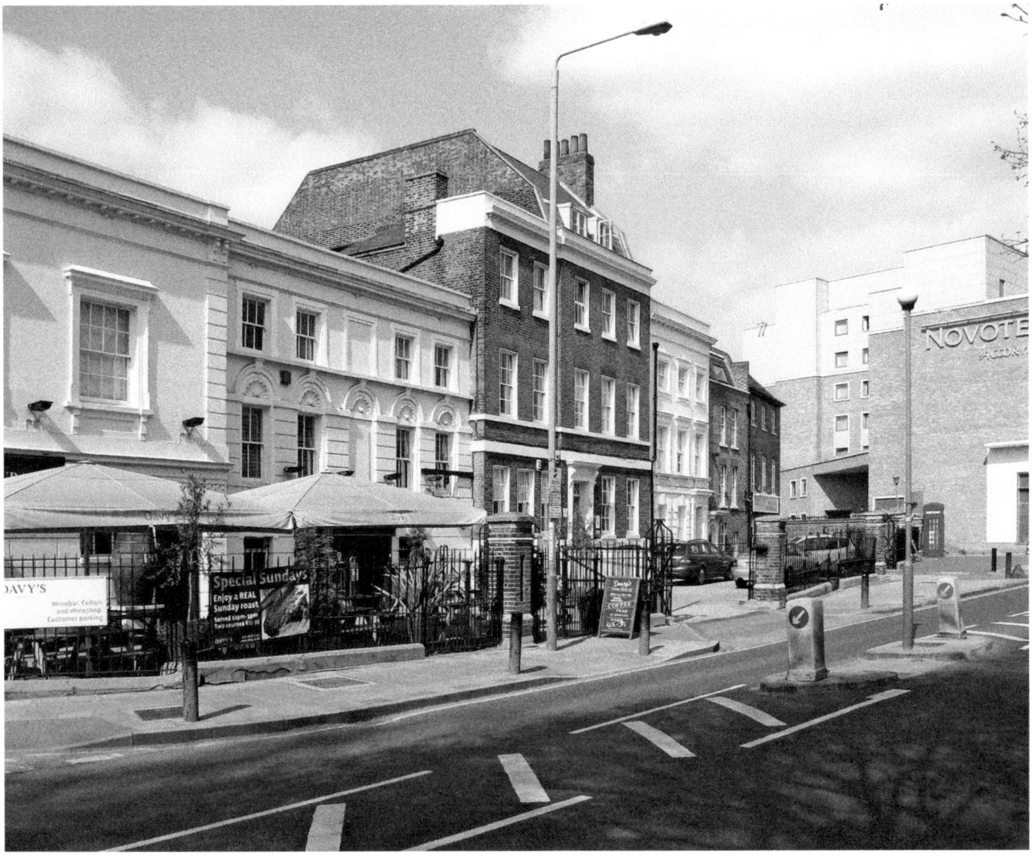


Davy's Wine Vault, Greenwich High Road, occupied up until 1968 by Lovibonds Brewery.

## MILLING, FARMING AND MANUFACTURING

Since the time of the Norman invasion a succession of tidal mills were situated along the River Ravensbourne, a tributary of the Thames, and it was not until the grain milling industry went through radical changes during the Industrial Revolution that tide mills, using traditional methods of milling by grindstone, were succeeded by steam-powered mills using new state-of-the-art steel rollers.

Two large brick-built mills which replaced Ravensbourne tidal mills, Mumford's and Robinson's, produced flour from grain brought up the Thames by barge from the fields of Kent and Essex. Although Mumford's Mill produced flour up until the mid-1900s, after the company was acquired by the Rank Group, now Rank Hovis, the building stood empty until converted into luxury apartments in the early twenty-first century. Robinson's Mill was demolished in 1970 after a fire raged through the building causing extensive damage.

During excavations for construction of a residential development at Lovell's Wharf in 2008, the remains of a twelfth-century tidal mill were revealed in the mud, believed to have been the first industrial structure built on Greenwich Marsh, and the earliest tidal mill discovered, to date, in London. To the south, high up on Blackheath, at least three windmills had once been

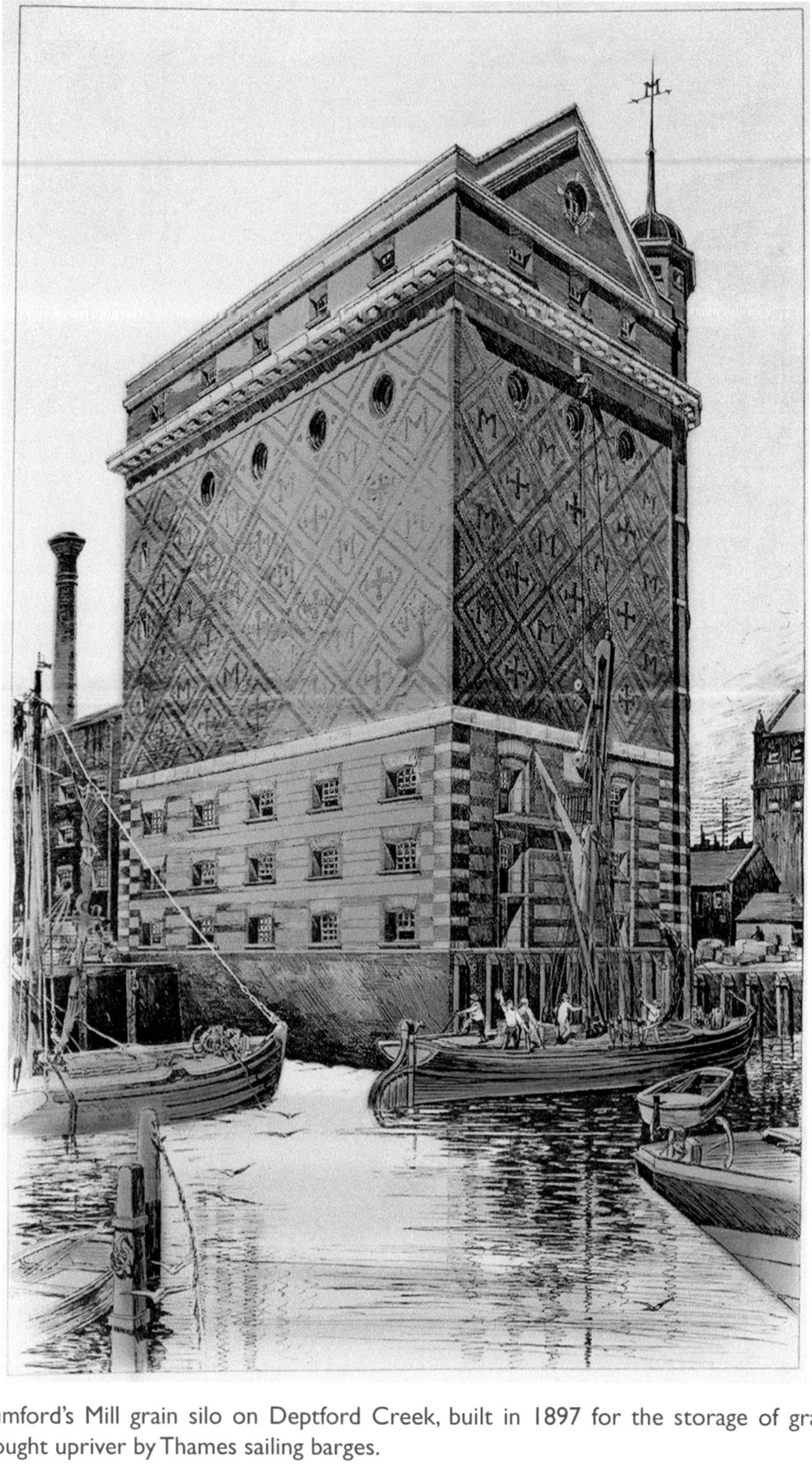

Mumford's Mill grain silo on Deptford Creek, built in 1897 for the storage of grain brought upriver by Thames sailing barges.

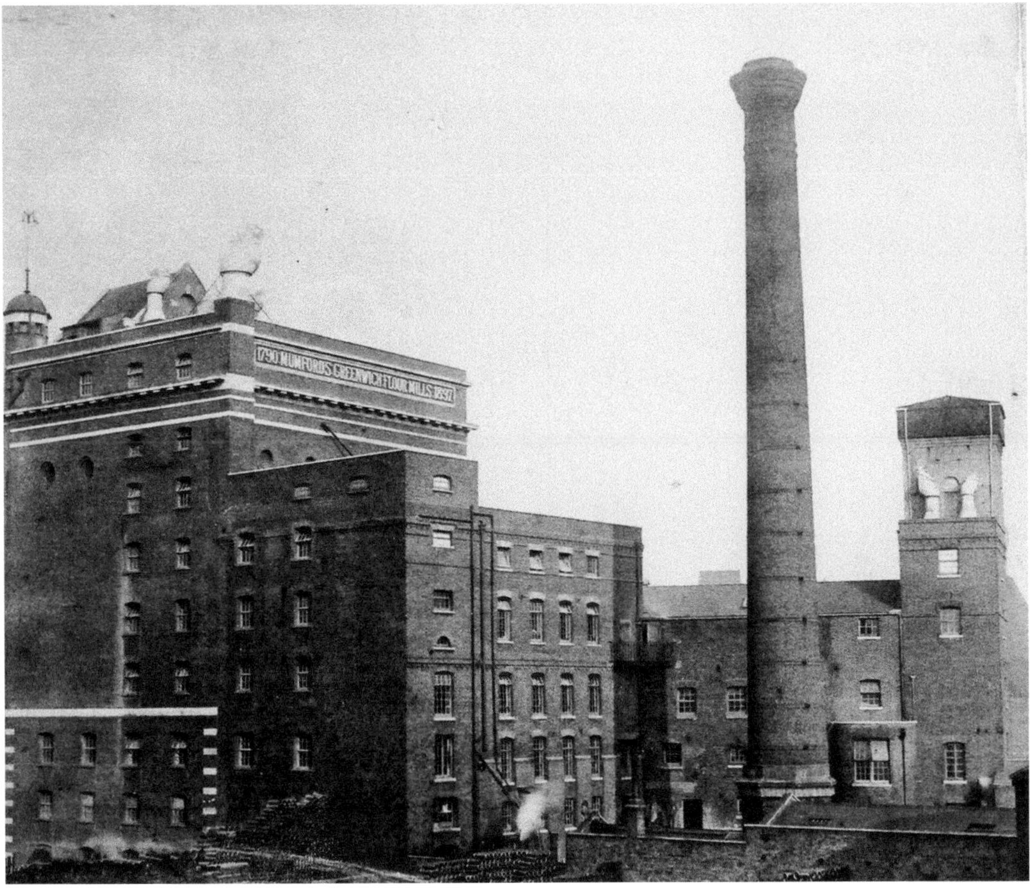


Erected on the site of a wooden tide mill in 1897, Mumford's Mill, along with the adjacent Robinson's Mill, offered employment to many local workers residing both sides of Deptford Creek.

in operation since the 1700s, one used to power a wood lathe, and much like tidal mills they were made redundant after the introduction of steam-powered mills.

Although a majority of grain came upriver from the farms of Essex and Kent, at one time Greenwich was surrounded by large areas of agricultural land, fields for crop growing and meadows for grazing. As Greenwich expanded outwards from the river, much of this land was taken over for erecting industrial buildings and workers' houses, many agricultural labourers taking up the offer of better-paid work in a variety of new industries.

A few market gardens continued growing crops and rearing livestock into the late 1800s, Combe Farm, situated to the east of the town centre, being one of the last. When Combe Farm was purchased by industrialist John Julius Angerstein in 1838, part of his Westcombe Park estate was leased out to the Roberts family, who continued to work the land on a much smaller scale as a market garden.

The farmhouse survived until 1901, when it was demolished to make way for Westcombe Park station and railway line, the farm labourers turning their hand to building a railway cutting through Combe Farm land.

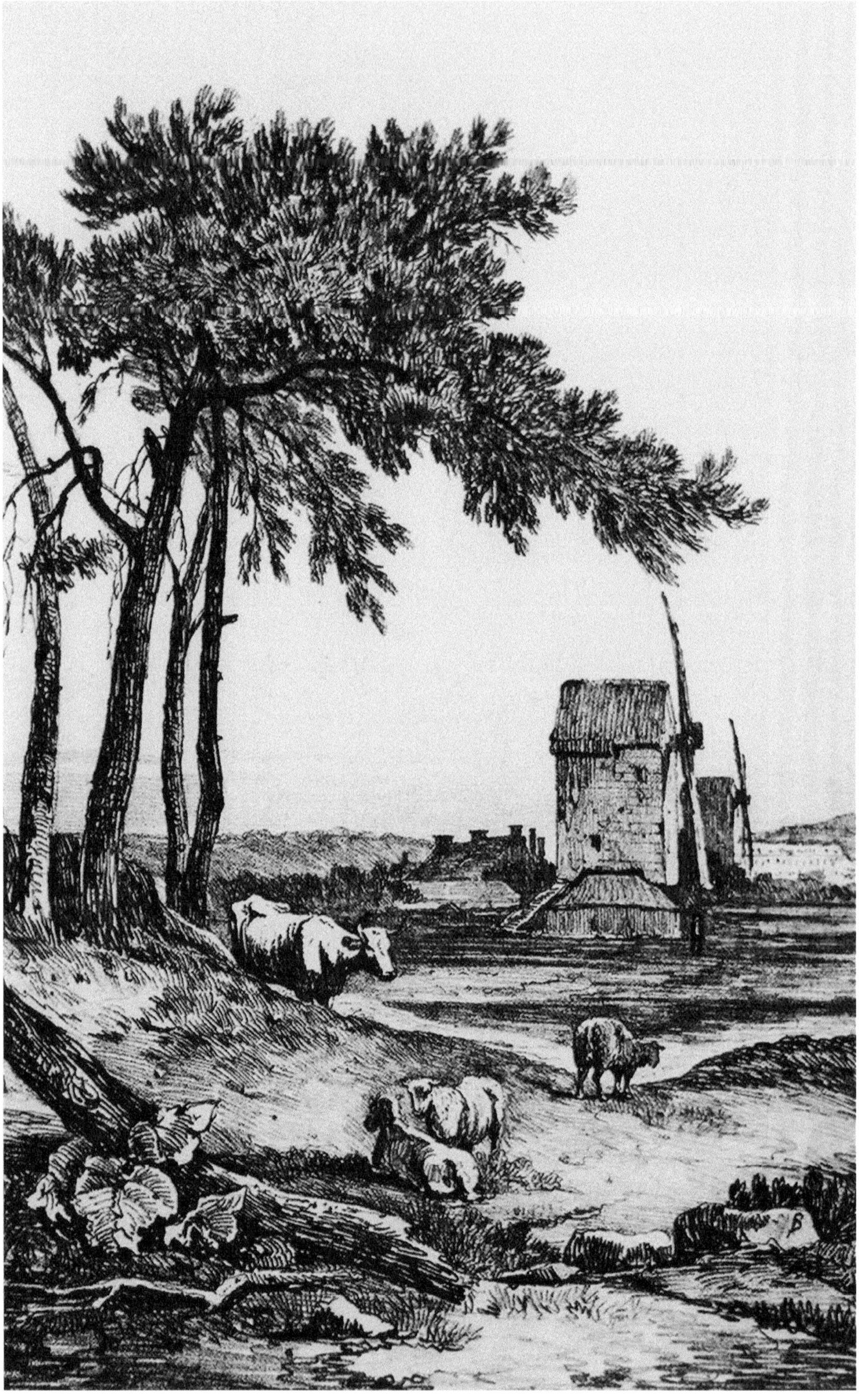

Blackheath windmills near Whitfield's Mount, early 1800s.

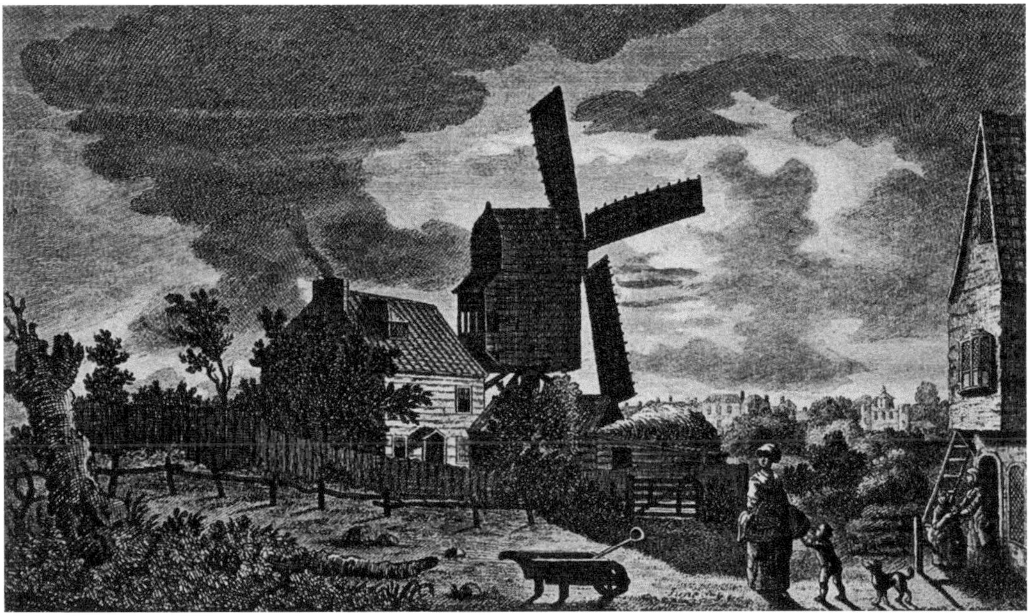

*Above*: Talbot Place Windmill on Blackheath, *c*. 1780.

*Right*: Combe Farm, late nineteenth century, land once owned by Anne Boleyn, a gift from Henry VIII.

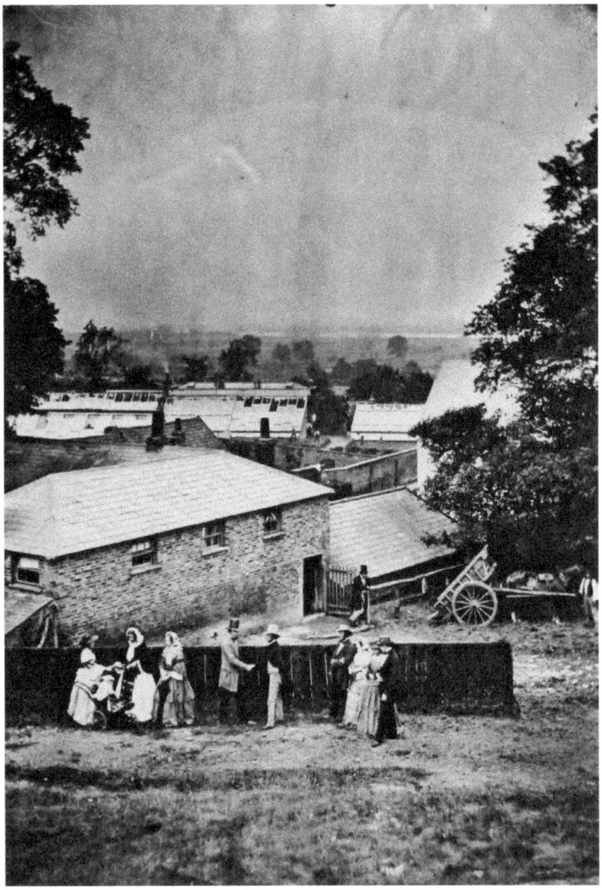

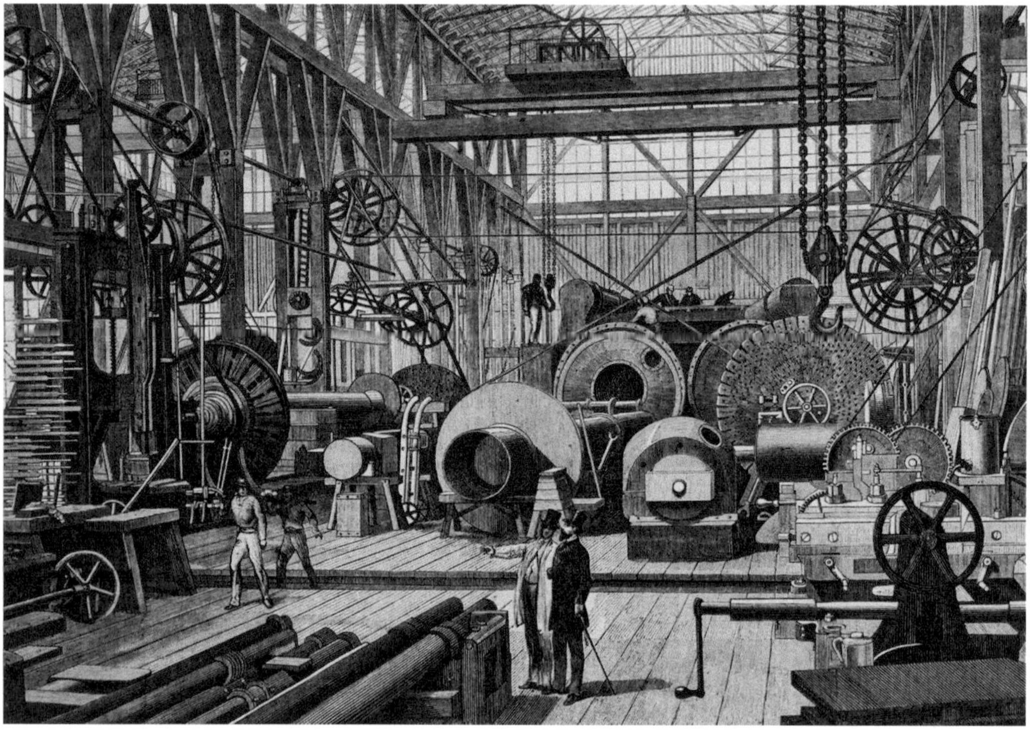

Penn's engineering works, Blackheath Road, reputed to have been the largest marine engine builders in the world.

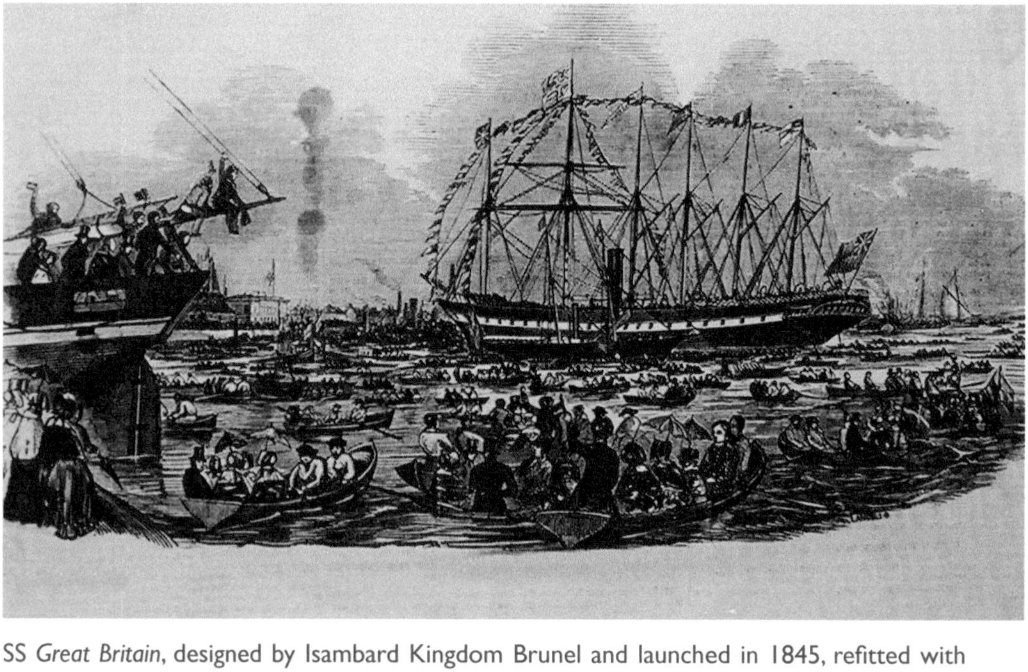

SS *Great Britain*, designed by Isambard Kingdom Brunel and launched in 1845, refitted with engines built by Penn's.

A further link to Greenwich farming heritage came through Devonshire-born John Penn, who established an engineering works in 1799 at the bottom of Blackheath Hill, close to Deptford Bridge, for the manufacture of agricultural machinery. After Penn's son, John, entered the family business, he began designing new types of steam engines. On inheriting the family business, he embarked on the design and manufacture of steam-powered marine engines, a time when the age of sail power was coming to an end.

The first Greenwich-built marine steam beam engines were fitted into paddle steamers *Ipswich* and *Suffolk* during the mid-1800s, and later, during a refurbishment of SS *Great Britain*, the ship's original engines were replaced with Penn's lighter and more efficient compact engines.

The Greenwich engineering works manufactured steam engines for over 700 vessels during John Penn's lifetime, and under the management of Penn's two sons, the company amalgamated with Thames Ironworks in 1899. After transferring business to Thames Ironworks north of the river, the Greenwich site closed, and the factory buildings were demolished.

A short distance from Penn's was Merryweather & Sons, on Greenwich High Road, manufacturers of fire appliances and fire engines. The company was established in 1692, at Longacre London, twenty-six years after the Great Fire.

The Greenwich workshop, which opened in 1876, employed many locals in the production of all types of steam-powered firefighting apparatus, compressors, water supply equipment and dredging apparatus. Merryweather & Sons constructed the very earliest hand-pushed firefighting appliances and horse-drawn fire engines, and later, through advancements made in design and engineering, self-propelled motorised fire engines and steam-powered fire boats. It was also reputed the company built the very first petrol driven car at the Greenwich works.

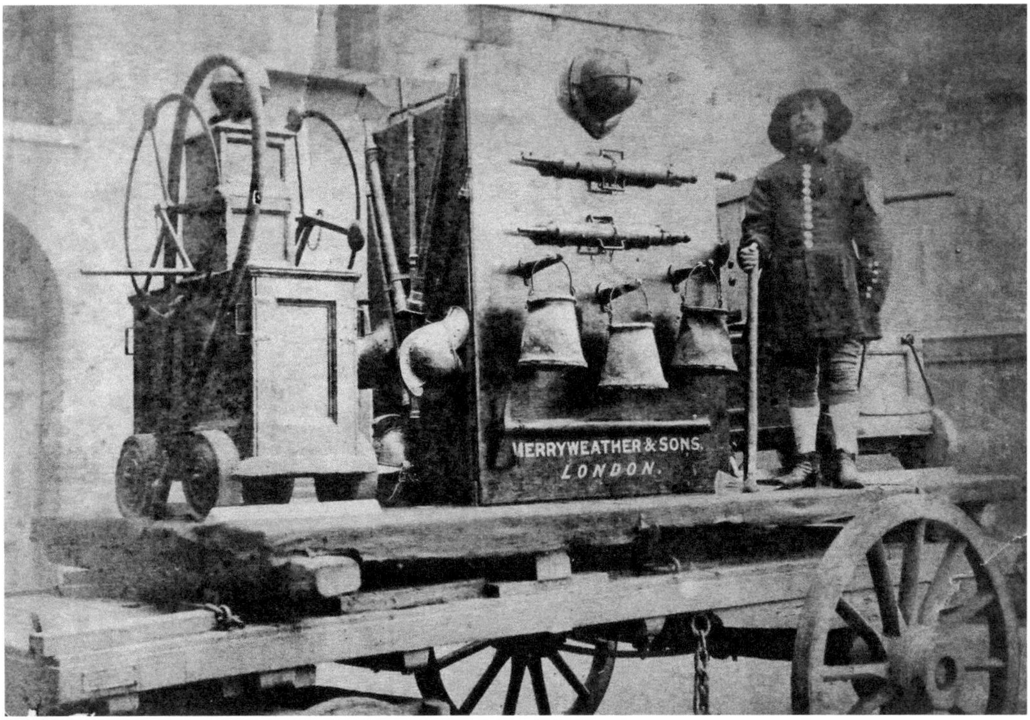


One of the first fire appliances made by Merryweather & Sons at their Greenwich works.

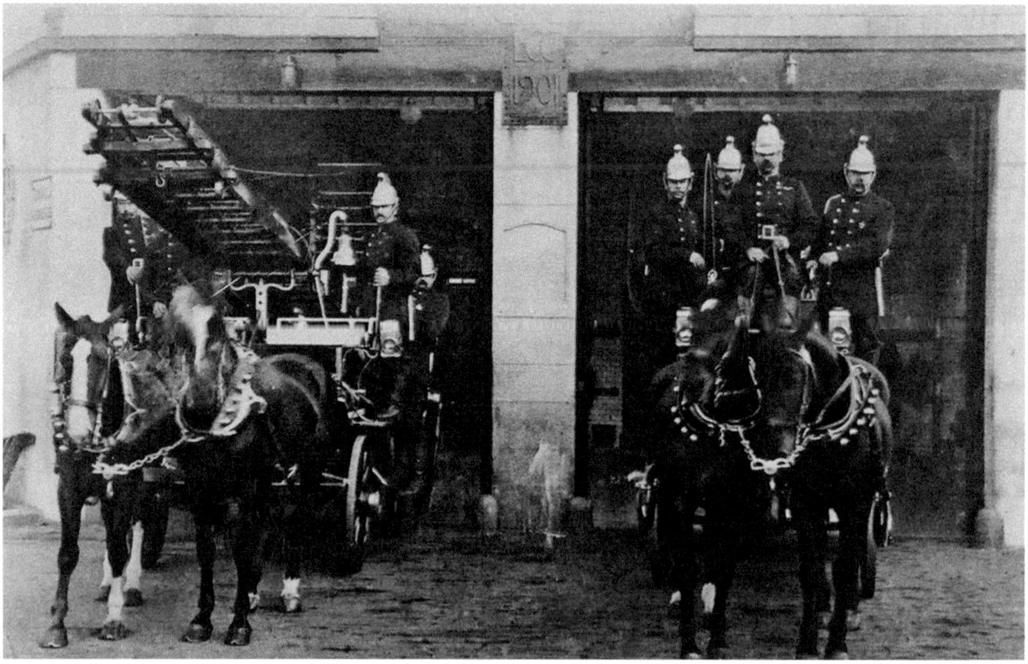

Greenwich Fire Brigade outside the East Greenwich fire station, early 1900s.

Merryweather fire engines were exported all around the world, including Australia, Brazil, China, India and New Zealand.

One of the Merryweather family members, Joe, joined the committee of a local boys' football club, Charlton Athletic, and after Woolwich Arsenal FC relocated to North London, Charlton rose up through the local football leagues. Drawing support from the workers of local industry, during the early 1900s, Charlton Athletic FC attracted crowds in excess of 60,000 for home games at their ground The Valley.

Merryweather & Sons continued producing firefighting equipment at Greenwich up until the 1960s, when the building was no longer fit for purpose and then demolished during the regeneration of the industrial areas of Greenwich in the early 2000s.

# PROTECTING PROPERTY

Most of London's first private fire brigades would have been equipped with Merryweather fire appliances, including the station at East Greenwich. Firemen at the time, a majority former sailors, earned between £1 to £1. 14 shillings per week to fight fires. After the Great Fire of London many properties were insured against fire, a metal plaque displayed on the building's front identifying the insurers to each private fire brigade.

In 1849, during the early hours one morning, a huge fire broke out in the premises of the Indian Rubber Works on Greenwich Street, the sole manufacturer of a new floor covering, a combination of cork and Indian rubber, Kamptulicon. So intense was the blaze that fire brigades from all over London were called upon to attended. Once the fire was extinguished it was discovered that one-hundred and fifty sheets of Kamptulicon stored in the loft of the fire ravaged building had been left almost undamaged, apart from some darkening by smoke. Experiments were then carried out by the Board of Admiralty at Woolwich Royal Dockyard to test the materials suitability for lining warship interiors as protection against fire breaking out from canon shots.

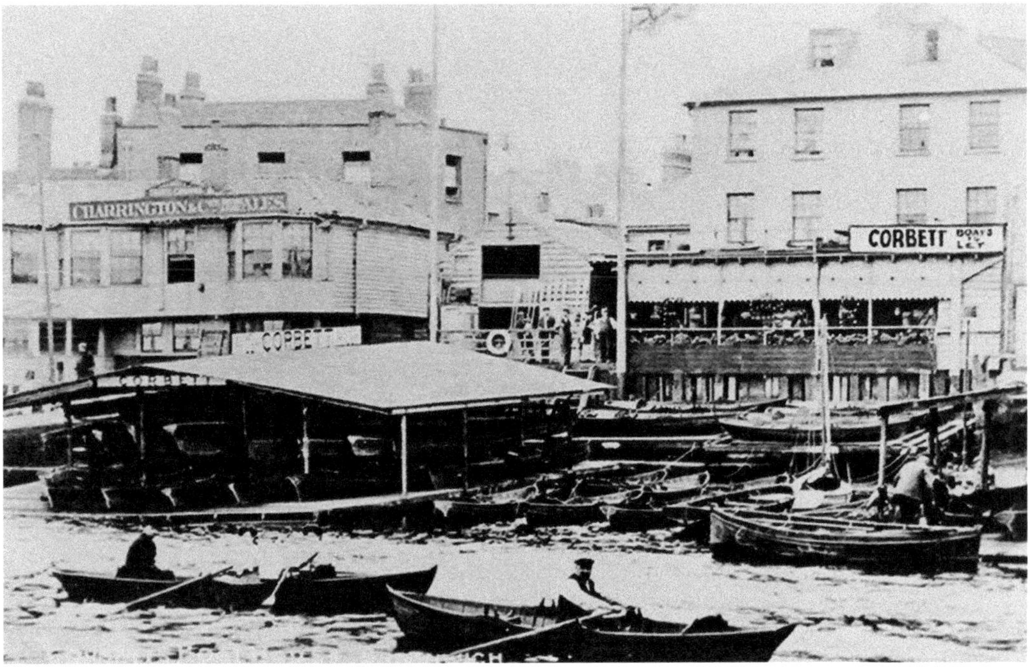


Corbett's Boatyard, off Crane Street, established during the early 1800s. Corbett's hired out all types of small rivercraft for work and pleasure.

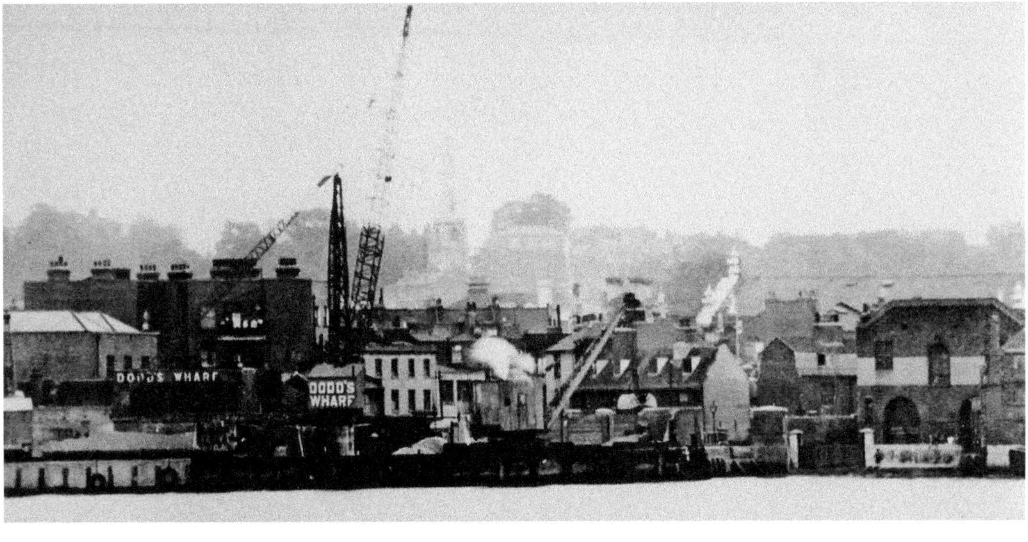


Dodds Wharf, to the east of Billingsgate Dock, c. 1937, occupied by general hauliers and Coneybeare engineers. (Greenwich Heritage Centre)

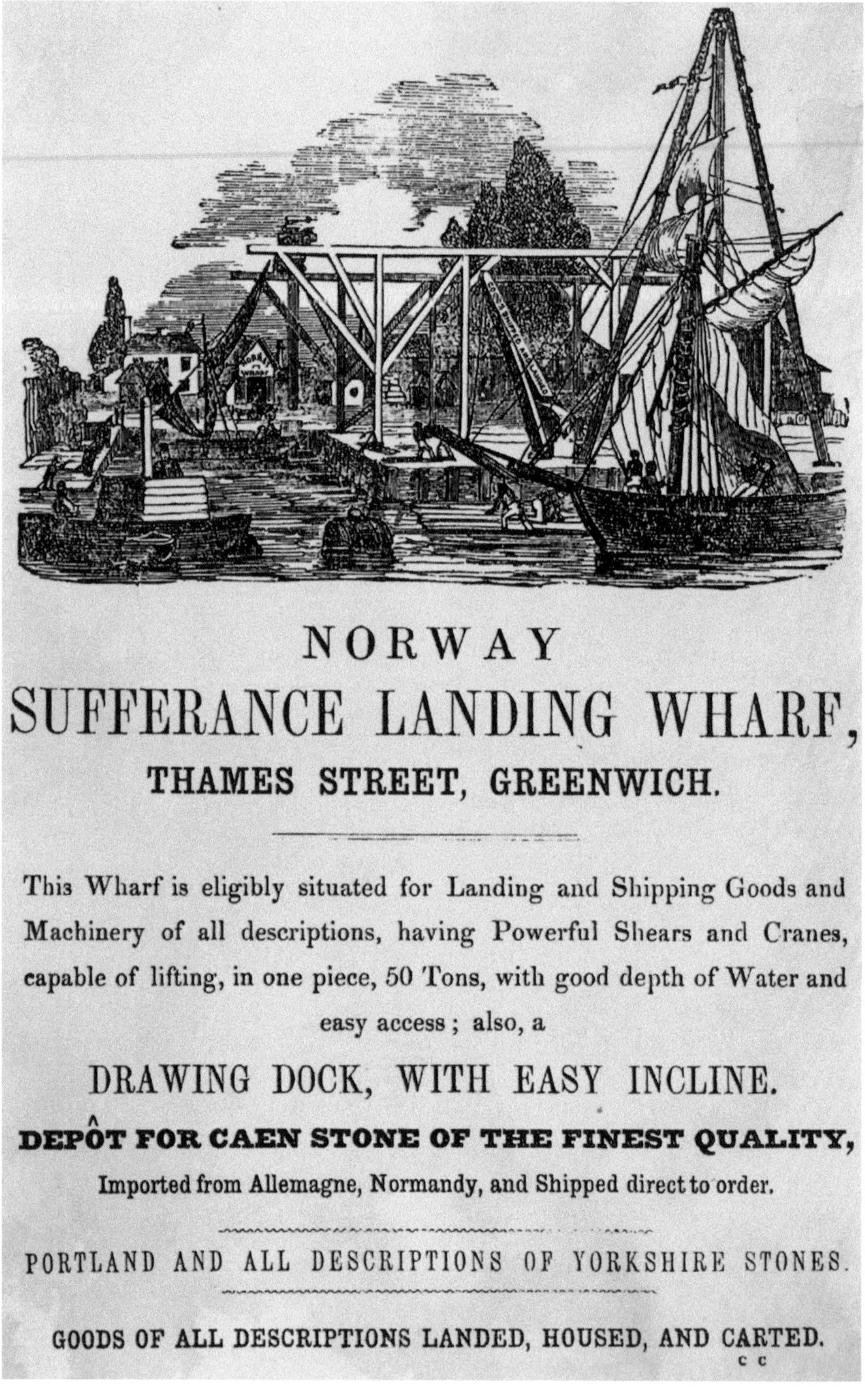


Norway Wharf advertisement from the late 1800s, where all types of goods were handled.

# RIVER POLICE AND PIRATES

Along the Greenwich waterfront there were many other small, but long-established, businesses and trades occupying riverside wharfs and yards, and with many ships, barges and lighters loaded with goods moored alongside, left unprotected awaiting unloading, it is of no surprise there was much river piracy carried out upon the Thames.

Under the cover of darkness, armed gangs raided the holds of ships berthed in the docks, or cut loose a barge or lighter from its riverside moorings, to let it drift downriver on an outgoing tide, the vessel later retrieved downstream and cargo removed undetected. Hundreds of thousands of pounds were lost annually through river piracy, a crime punished by hanging. Pirates found guilty would be hanged at Execution Dock, Wapping, the lifeless corpse then taken downstream to Blackwall Point and left to hang on a gibbet, serving as a warning to other river pirates.

In 1798, a Marine Police Force was established by Master Mariner John Harriott and magistrate Patrick Colquhoun, to combat the theft and looting of goods from ships, barges and lighters, the Marine Police predating the Metropolitan Police Force by just over thirty years. At the outset, the Marine Police, numbering just fifty – many former Royal Navy men – were stationed at Wapping. The force soon increased to around 200 officers. In the first year of operation over £120,000 of goods had been saved from theft, worth around £100,000,000 today.

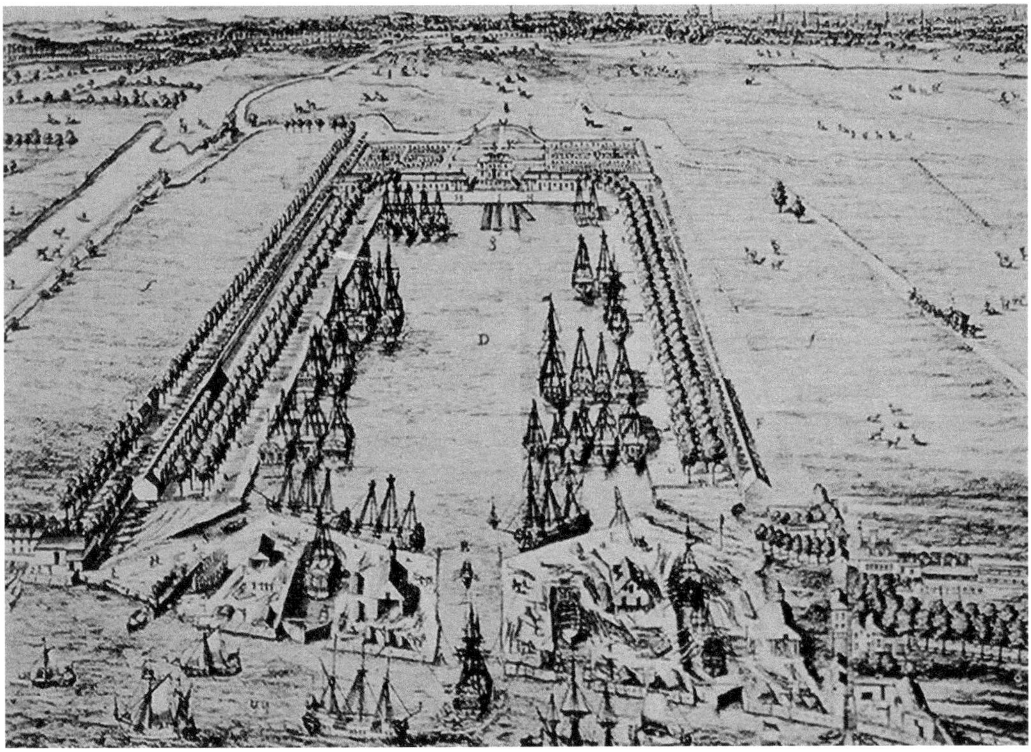

Howland Wet Dock, laid out between 1695 and 1699, the oldest of all London's riverside docks. Located to the north of Deptford Dockyard, the wet dock was used for berthing and repairing East India traders and later Greenland whalers, the name changing to Greenland Dock.

It has been reported that the last hanging of a corpse at Blackwall Point took place in 1834, close to where the Marine Police stationed one of two floating police stations. The first, former Royal Naval prison hulk HMS *Tower*, was a six-gun tender launched in 1809, moored to the west of Greenwich Marsh.

Retired from service in 1826, the hulk was later replaced by HMS *Royalist* under the command of Inspector Bliss, who lived aboard ship. The Marine Police included ship constables to supervise the dockworkers, their wages paid for by the shipowners; police surveyors, visiting vessels to check the loading and unloading of cargo; police watermen, rowing the police galleys; and a Surveyor of Quays and police quay guards, engaged to watch over cargo on shore.

Another important duty of the force included rescuing people who fell into the Thames and searching for and dealing with the bodies of suicides, murder victims, and those who drowned accidentally, the police rowing to incidents in galleys. After the collision between *Princess Alice* and *Bywell Castle* off Woolwich, where over 600 people lost their lives, the inquest recommended the Thames Division, a merger between the Marine Police and Metropolitan Police, should be equipped with hired steam launches to attend incidents more speedily.

These steam launches were found to be unreliable and the force carried on using rowing galleys, a few of which were later motorised. These galleys were replaced by petrol- and paraffin-fuelled launches, succeeded during the 1920s by diesel engine boats, the Thames Division patrolling the tidal river from Teddington Locks in Surrey to Dartford Creek in Kent, a length of 36 miles.

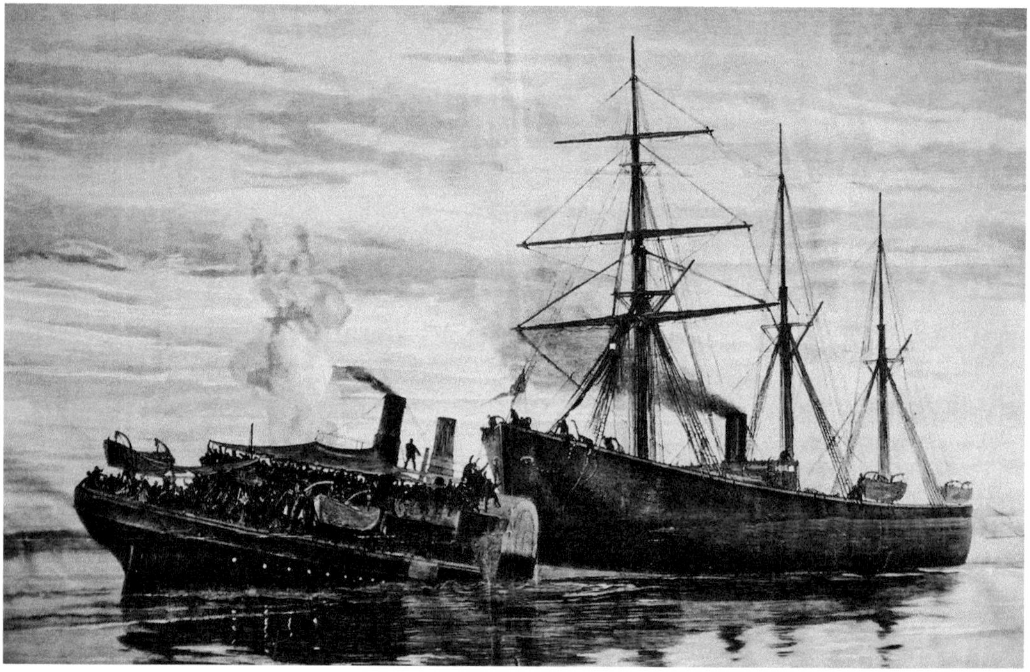

Passenger paddle steamer *Princess Alice* and steam collier *Bywell Castle* collide at Gallions Reach, September 1878. (Greenwich Heritage Centre)

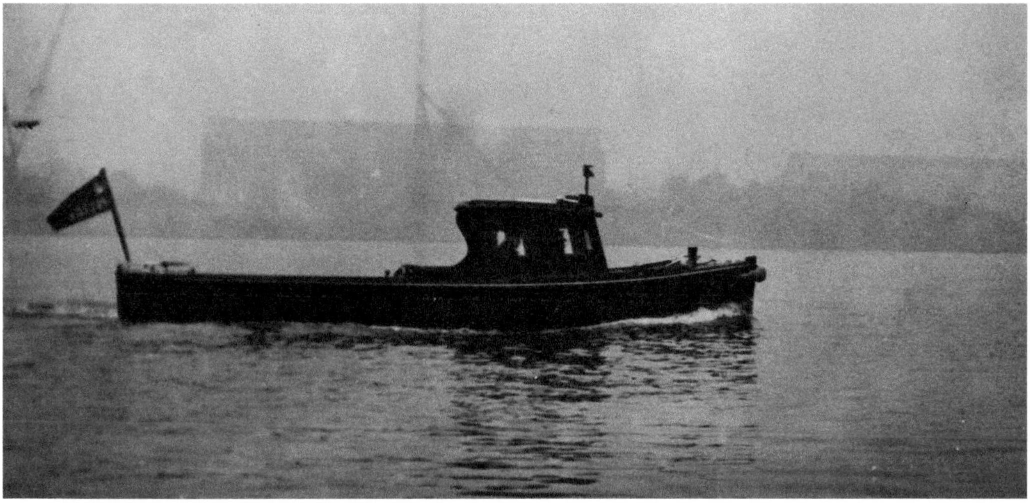

Thames Division police launch mid-1900s.

## PATROLLING THE STREETS OF A WORKING TOWN

Following the formation of both the Metropolitan Police and the City of London Police, the number of officers in London during the latter part of the 1800s, including the Thames Division, amounted to around 16,000 men and at least twenty women, who were employed as matrons to guard women and children. The Metropolitan Police was divided into divisions, each identified by a letter. By 1869, Greenwich R Division comprised of a force including a superintendent in charge of the division, eleven inspectors overseeing subdivisions, forty-eight sergeants of sections, and 362 constables patrolling designated beats.

The very first Greenwich police station was situated at the aptly named Cut Throat Lane, opposite present-day Greenwich railway station, the building consisting simply of a lock-up known as the Cage.

The main divisional police station was located at Blackheath Road, operational from 1841. The station was then rebuilt in 1909, and as other local stations opened throughout the division, as the force grew in numbers, the area of operation encompassed Deptford to the west, Woolwich through to Erith in the east, and as far south as Chislehurst. Police stations were also situated in the dockyards of Deptford and Woolwich, as well as at the Royal Arsenal, to combat the theft of goods and materials. Primarily the work of the force was to patrol and safeguard property and persons. The main offenders officers had to deal with were thieves and drunkards, followed by receivers of stolen goods, prostitutes, vagrants and tramps. Assaults and murders were, if not rare, infrequent.

Police officers were sent out to patrol their designated beats with a truncheon for protection and a rattle to signal for help, the rattle later replaced by the police officers' distinctive-sounding whistles. Basic pay for police officers during the late 1800s amounted to around 10 shillings per week, plus allowances for coal, uniform and medical care. The weekly wage rose to £1 for good conduct. Selection to the force was strict, with only 25 per cent of applicants meeting the obligatory standards, which included proving to be physically fit, of an age between twenty to twenty-seven years, and a minimum height of 5 feet 9 inches – this was prior to passing a mandatory exam.

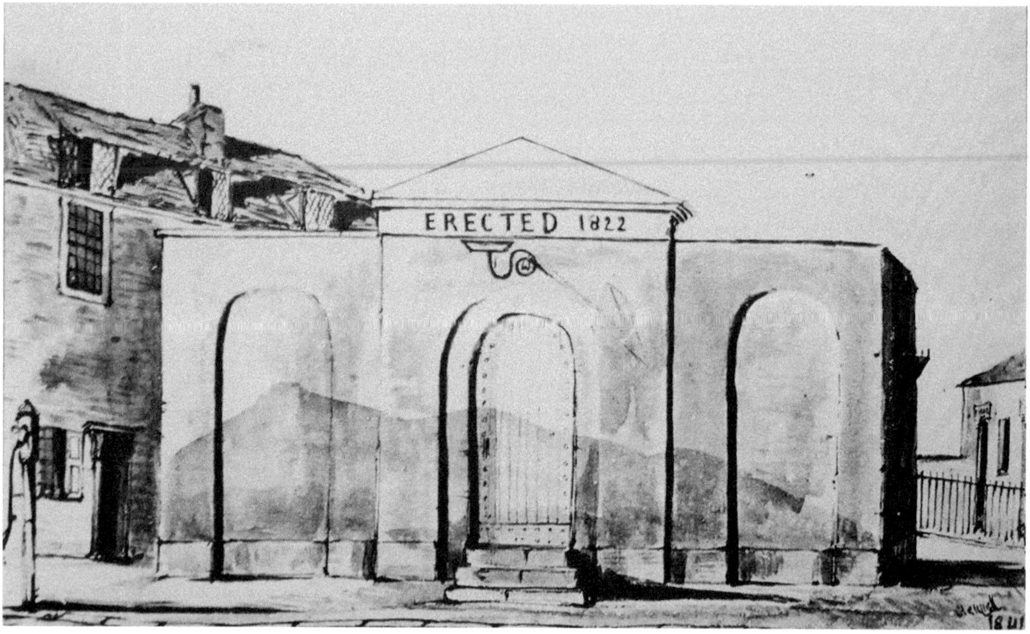


Greenwich lock-up known as The Cage, *c.* 1822.

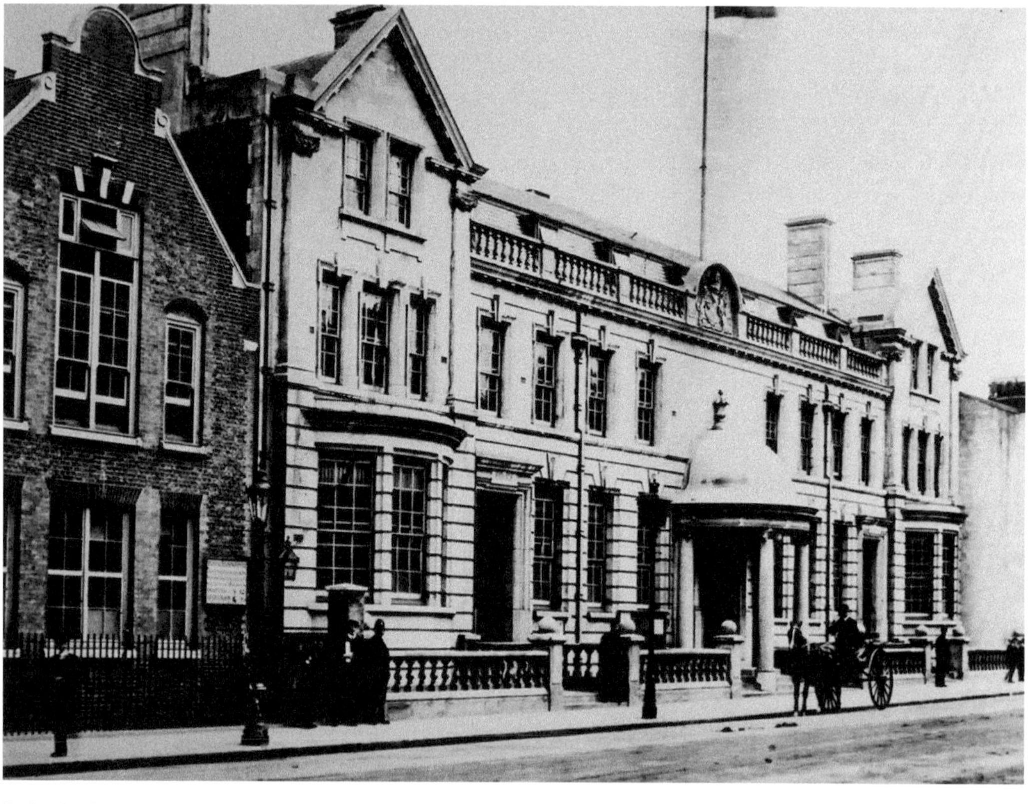

Rebuilt Greenwich Police Station and Magistrates' Court, Blackheath Road, early 1900s.

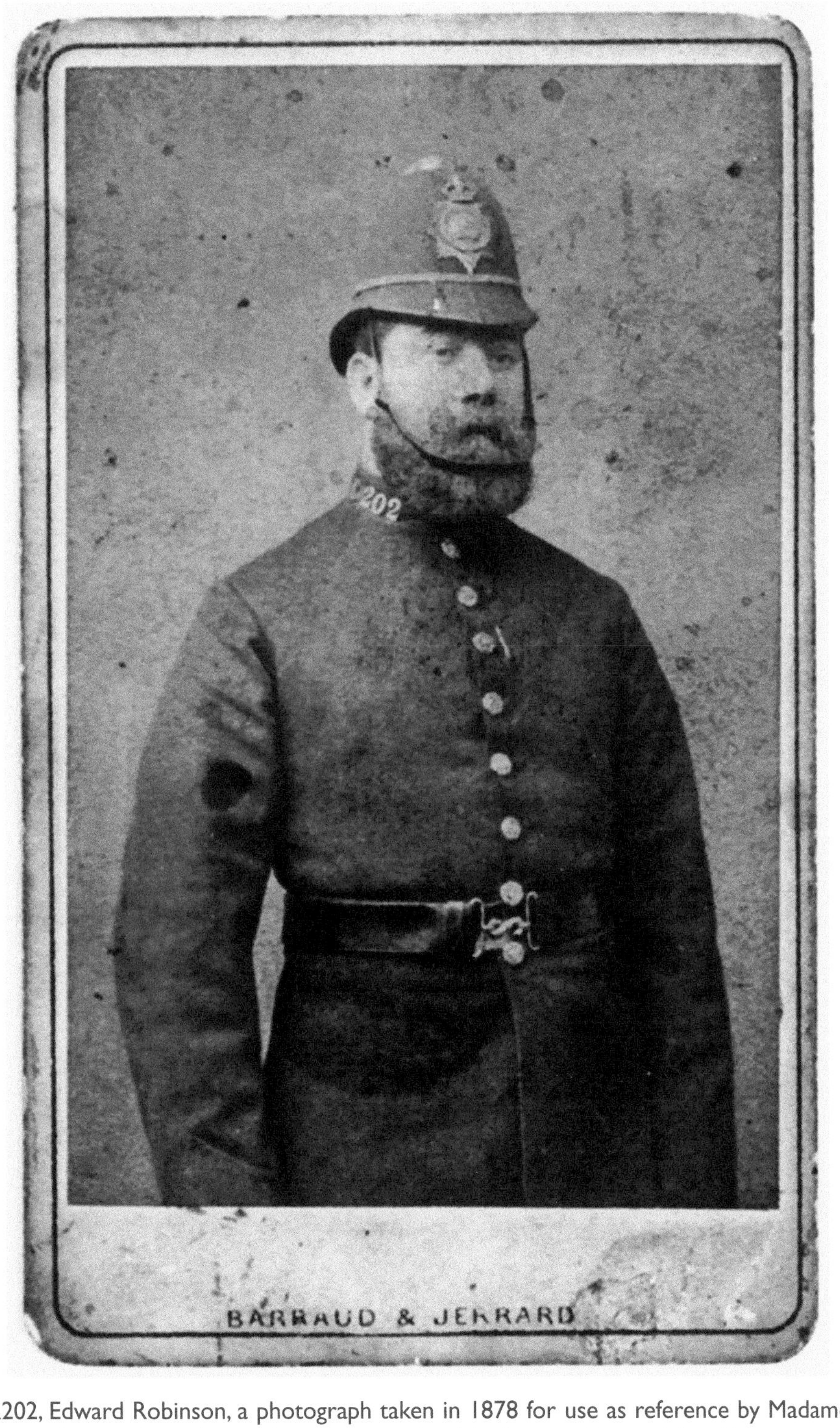


R202, Edward Robinson, a photograph taken in 1878 for use as reference by Madame Tussauds modelers when making a waxwork of the famous Greenwich policeman.

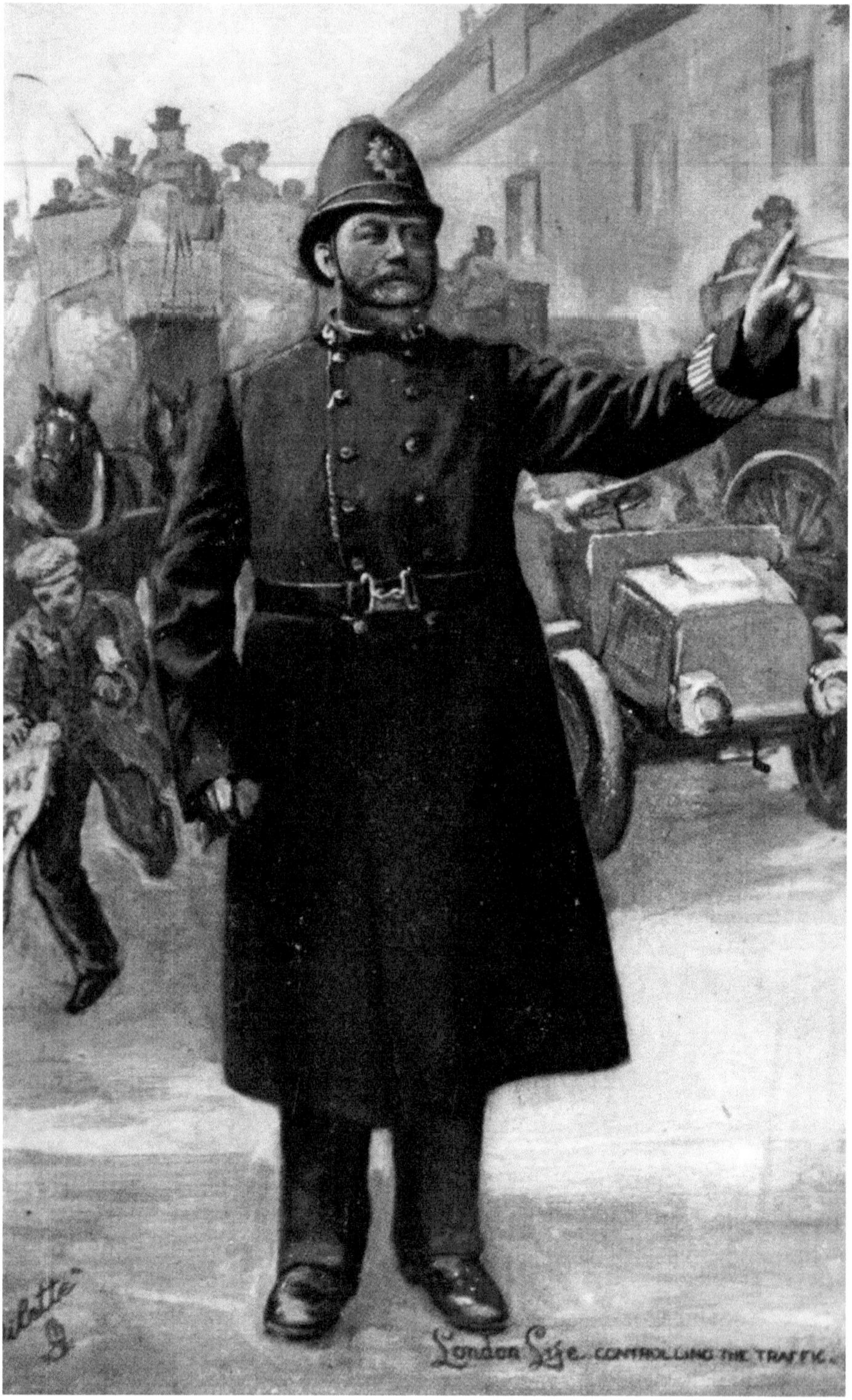


Portrait of a Metropolitan 'Bobby' controlling the traffic, *c.* 1905 – very similar in appearance to PC Edward Robinson.

My great-great uncle, Edward Robinson, joined the police force in 1870, at the age of twenty-two, and was stationed at R Division. Police Constable Edward Robinson, Divisional Number R202, was a large burly chap who became a well-respected and well-recognised figure in the community, even more so following his apprehension of Charles Peace when the Victorian master criminal attempted to make his escape after burgling a house at Blackheath. The local police force became so efficient at their job that they were tasked to carry out other duties including searching for missing persons, taking injured people to hospital for treatment, directing traffic and crowd control.

## INNOVATIVE INDUSTRY AND TRADITIONAL PRACTICES

Greenwich industry was well recognised for new innovations in technological manufacturing, especially in the field of communications, not only developed at Glass, Elliott & Co., makers of revolutionary submarine telegraph cables (the company merging with the Telegraph Construction and Maintenance Company), but also at Siemens, situated between Charlton and Woolwich, founded by William Siemens in 1858. Siemens designed and manufactured various types of revolutionary telegraphy cables, electrical cables and components.

German-born William formed a partnership with his older brother, Ernst Werner von Siemens, founder of Berlin-based Siemens & Halske, and although there were some initial setbacks in the production of electric cables, by 1863 the factory expanded to cover around 6 acres, employing over 2,000 workers under the new title Siemens Brothers.

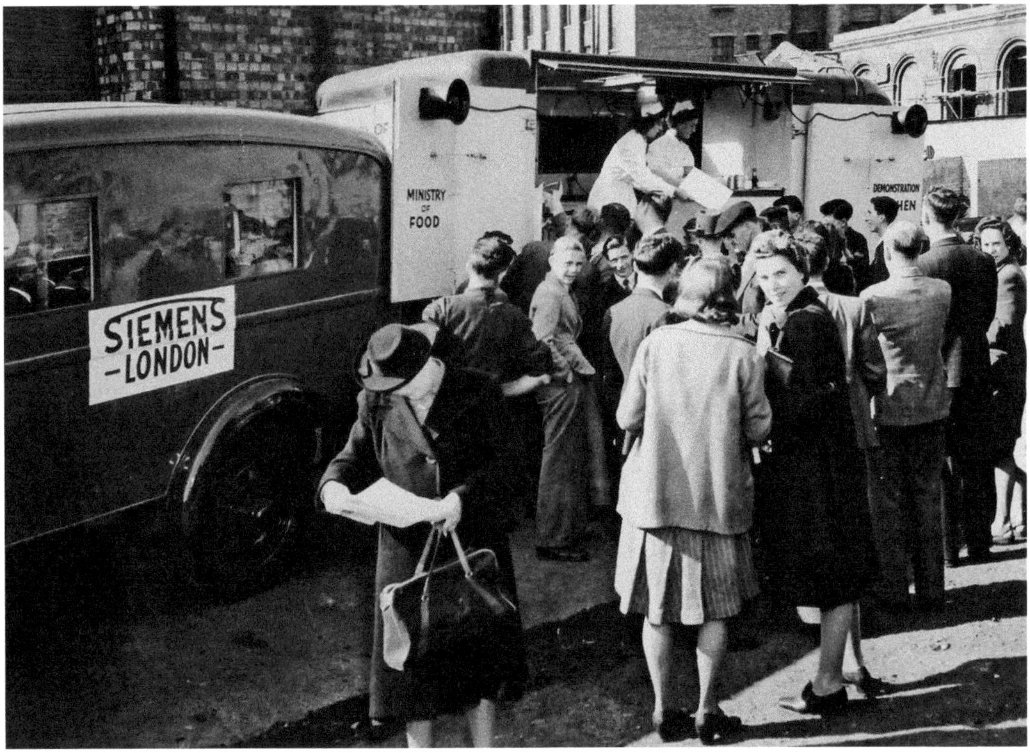


A Ministry of Food mobile kitchen is holding a demonstration outside Siemens telegraph factory, Lower Charlton, showing workers how to make the most of food rations.

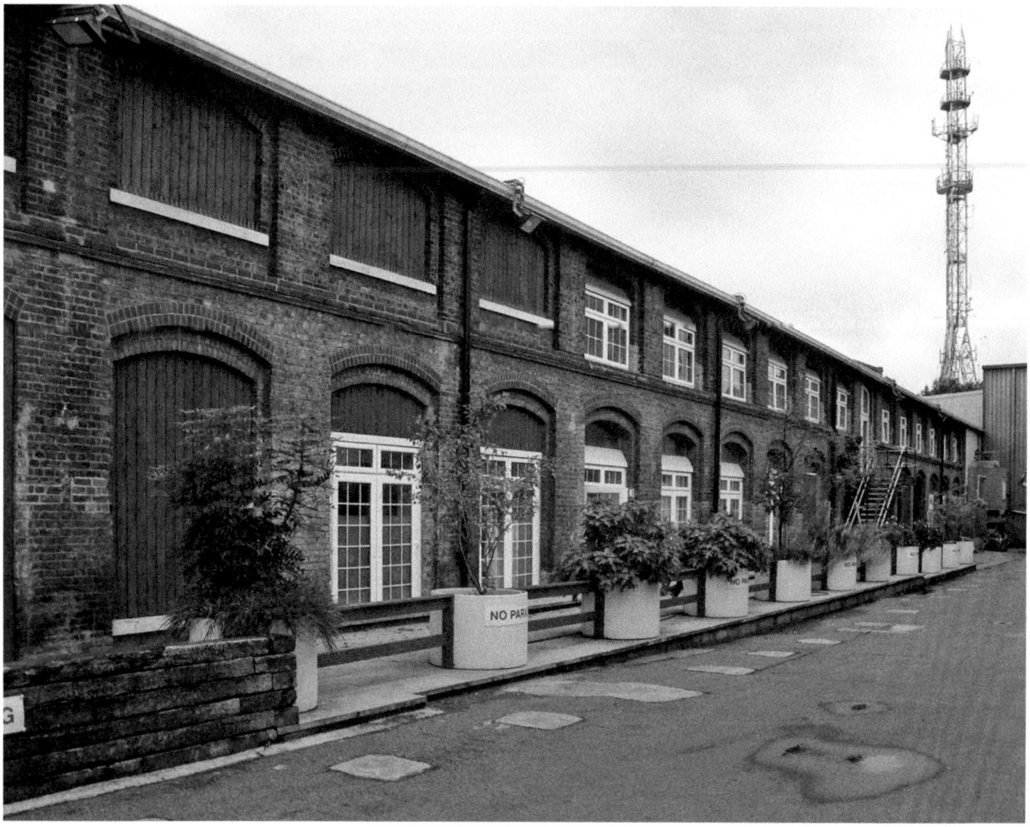

Former Siemens factory buildings close to the Thames are now studios and workshops occupied by artists and craftspeople, designers, printers and photographers.

The company went on to successfully make and lay thousands of miles of electronic communication cables around the globe. Siemens' apprentice, Liverpool-born Sebastian de Ferranti, went on to design the first high-voltage power station, erected at Deptford East and opened in 1899. During the First World War, the company, then mostly owned by German nationals, was bought by a British consortium under the Trading with the Enemy Act 1914, and the factory went on to design and make a fuel pipeline, code named PLUTO, pumping petrol from England to France to supply vehicles of the Allied invasion force in the Second World War.

The factory closed in 1968, as the aged buildings were no longer fit for purpose, leaving some 6,000 workers unemployed one year after the Royal Ordnance works at Woolwich Royal Arsenal also shut down, which brought financial and social hardship to the local area. Although some of the original Siemens industrial buildings which survived the bombing raids of the Second World War are considered to be of historic industrial importance, several refurbished for use as studio space, others are under threat of demolition for the erection of new residential properties.

At one time there would have been many small family-run businesses and independent trades located between rows of terraced properties throughout Greenwich, at the end of cul-de-sacs, or squeezed in between large commercial buildings. These trades and businesses consisted of blacksmiths, coopers, wheelwrights, millwrights, engineers, carriage works, printers, bookbinders, road haulage depots, farriers, dairies, wood merchants, foundries and stonemasons, to name just a few.

One small industry located near St Alfege Church, Workshops for the Blind of Kent, founded by Major General Bainbrigge, provided training and employment for the blind. Here, workers made all types of household and commercial goods, such as rugs, baskets, ships' fenders and ropework.

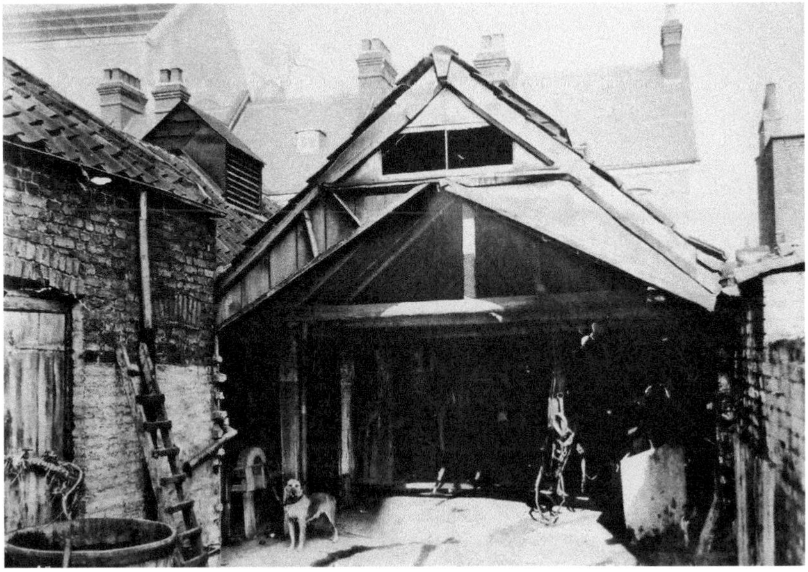

Stable yard south of Greenwich Power Station, one of many during the early 1900s stabling cart pulling horses of local tradesmen.

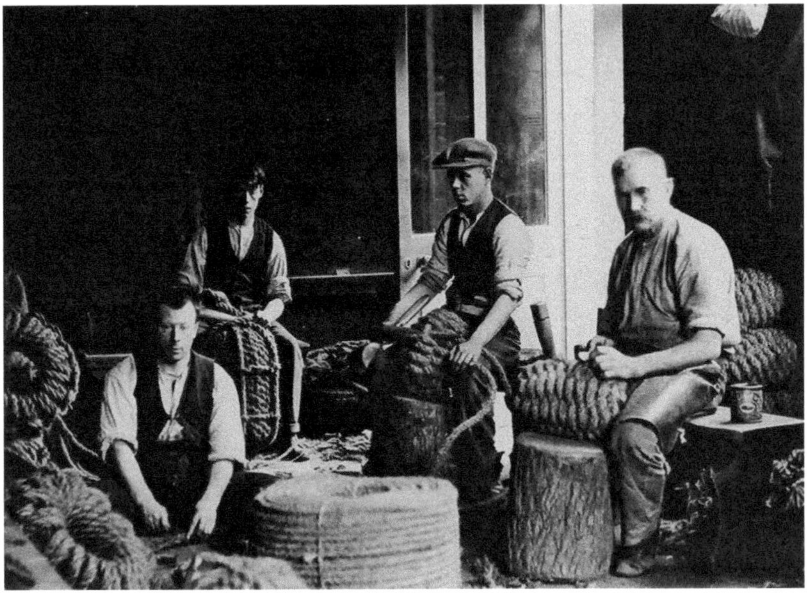

Workshops for the Blind of Kent, located on the corner of Stockwell Street, early 1900s.

Brookes Crystals Ltd, on Stockwell Street, produced and supplied crystals (electronic valves) for aircraft and marine transmitters; William A. Halstead, of Derwent Street, manufactured paste distemper used for covering hospital walls and ceilings; F. J. Mee made model aeroplanes at Greenwich Road; T. W. Thompson & Co., Blissett Street, manufactured ignition coils; P.A. Carter & Sons, motor engineers and hauliers, had a depot at Christ Church Way; Robinson's Iron and Metal Merchants, based at Anchor Iron Wharf, dealt in the purchase and sale of various scrap metals; British Acoustic Co., located at Church Street, patented and manufactured electrical and non-electrical instruments for the deaf; W. A. Willson's Mineral Waters, at Eastney Street, made soft drinks; and A. Haysome & Son, at Annandale Road, were monumental masons.

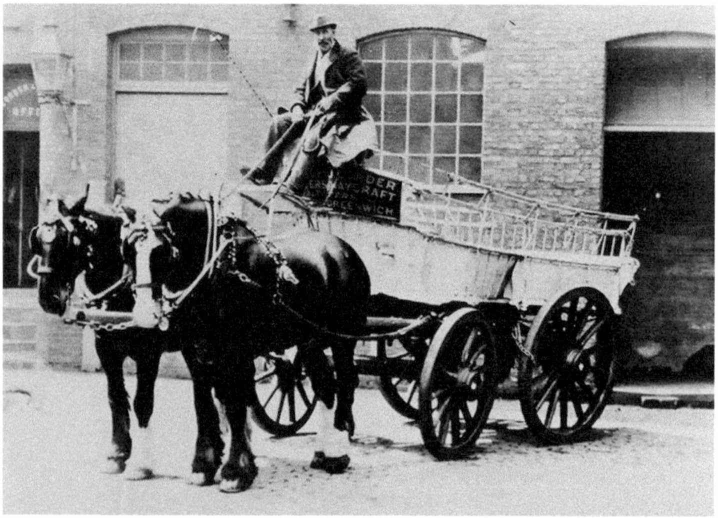

Horse and dray of maltsters Corder & Haycraft, a jointly owned small business with malting kilns situated to the rear of the Spread Eagle coaching Inn off Nevada Street, late 1800s.

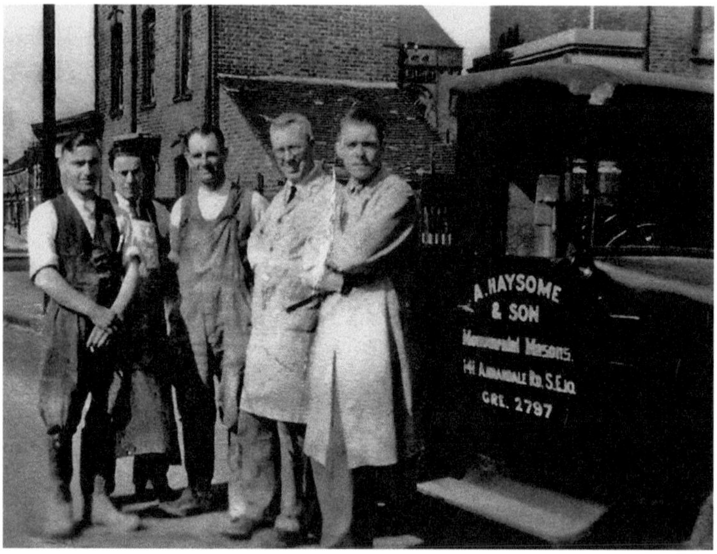


Workers from A. Haysome & Son. George Cooper, far right, a Haysome's apprentice, served with the Royal Engines during the Second World War. After rejoining Haysome's, he took up employment at Greenwich Gasworks Fuel Research department, Blackwall Lane. (Roger Cooper)

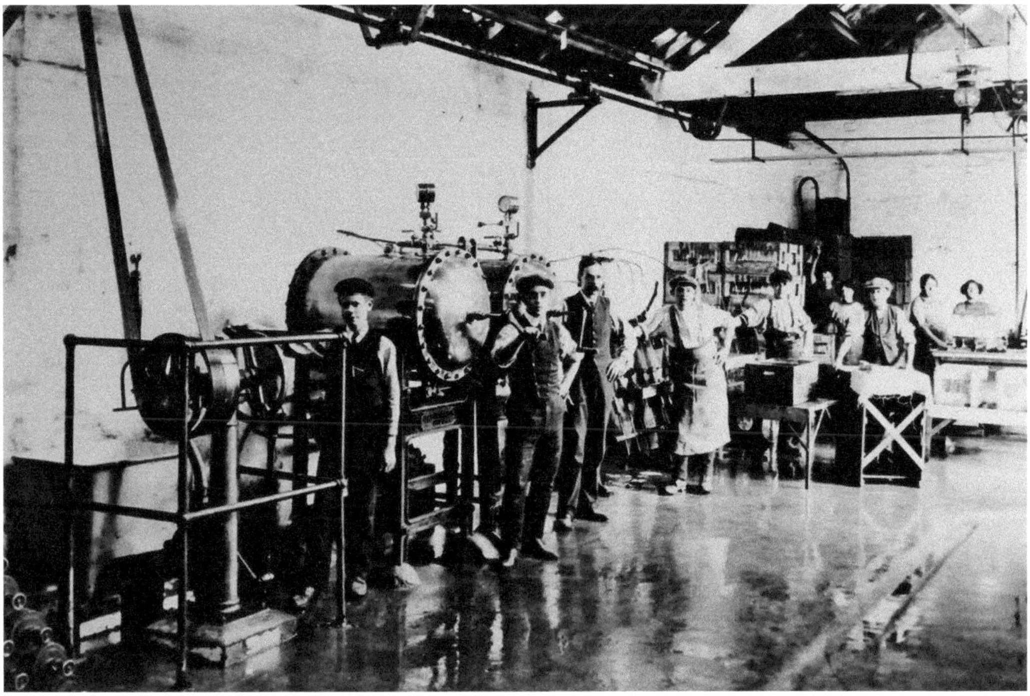

W.A. Willson's production line, Eastney Street, *c.* 1906, where workers were first employed bottling mineral water before making and bottling lemonade, ginger beer and cola, the beginnings of the soft drinks industry.

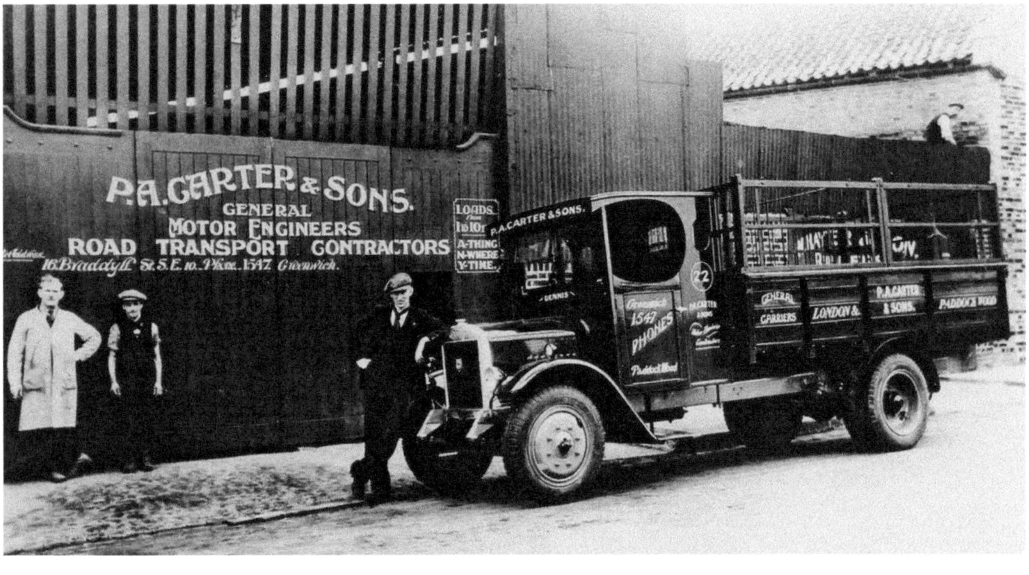


Motor engineers P.A. Carter & Sons, early 1900s. From a small family-run motor engineering business, by the mid-twentieth century Carter's expanded operations into road haulage, equipped with a fleet of fifty-eight vehicles and various low-loaders, semi-low-loaders and specialist trailers.

And there were many Greenwich residents and business entrepreneurs who had interesting occupations during the age of industrialisation: George Delianson Clark, inventor's agent; Alexander Duckham, oil merchant; William Tutin Haycraft, MD., patentee; John Steers, lime burner; David Batchelor, analyst; John Coneybeare, sausage machine manufacturer; Thomas Corden, inspector of nuisances and Edwin Theobald, magical apparatus maker.

## COMMUTER TRAFFIC

To transport workers to and from their places of work, when the only options were either walking or riding a bike (travelling by horse and carriage then a privilege of the wealthy), horse-pulled trams were introduced into Greenwich by an Act of Parliament in 1880 after the formation of the Woolwich and Plumstead Tramway Company in 1879. When taken over by a local businessman in 1881, a new company was established, the Woolwich and South-East London Tramways Company, and the tramway was extended from Woolwich to Greenwich, joining end on to tracks of the London Tramways Company.

Many of the horses-pulling tramcars were stabled at Greenwich, at the site of the demolished house of Iron Master Sir Ambrose Crowley, whose foundry made ships' anchors and shackles and chains for the slave trade. The site was then used for the building of Greenwich Power Station supplying electricity to the new electrified tram system. In 1904, London County Council took control of the transport system, replacing horse-drawn tramcars with electrified trams; the service continued transporting workers back and forth to their places of employment for almost fifty years. Trams were eventually replaced by electric-powered trolleybuses and motor buses, the redundant trams ending their days at the breakers' yard in Charlton.

Electrification also came to London's first steam passenger railway, the Greenwich to London Bridge line, which by the late 1800s had extended to Central London terminals and outwards into Kent, the expansion of the railway system providing workers with an opportunity to commute to work from further out in the suburbs. As the railway services expanded operations, many local branch lines were opened, although not all were successful. The branch line from Nunhead to Greenwich, fully operational by 1888, had closed to passenger services by 1917, as a wartime economy measure.

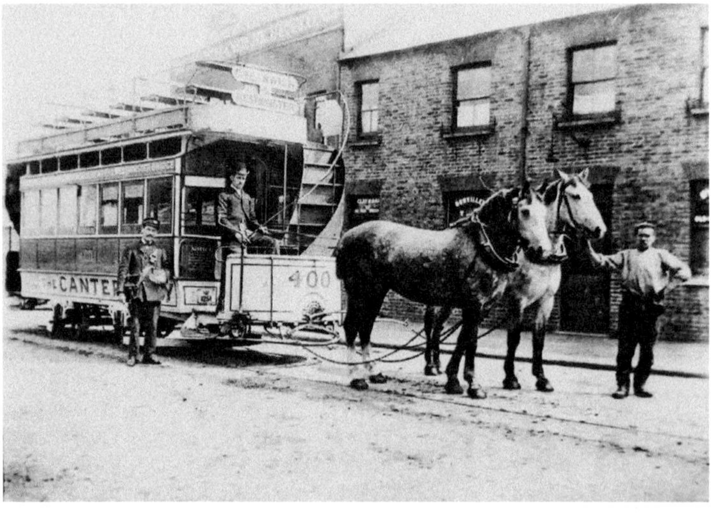


One of the first horse-drawn Greenwich trams, c. 1890, outside the Star & Garter public house.

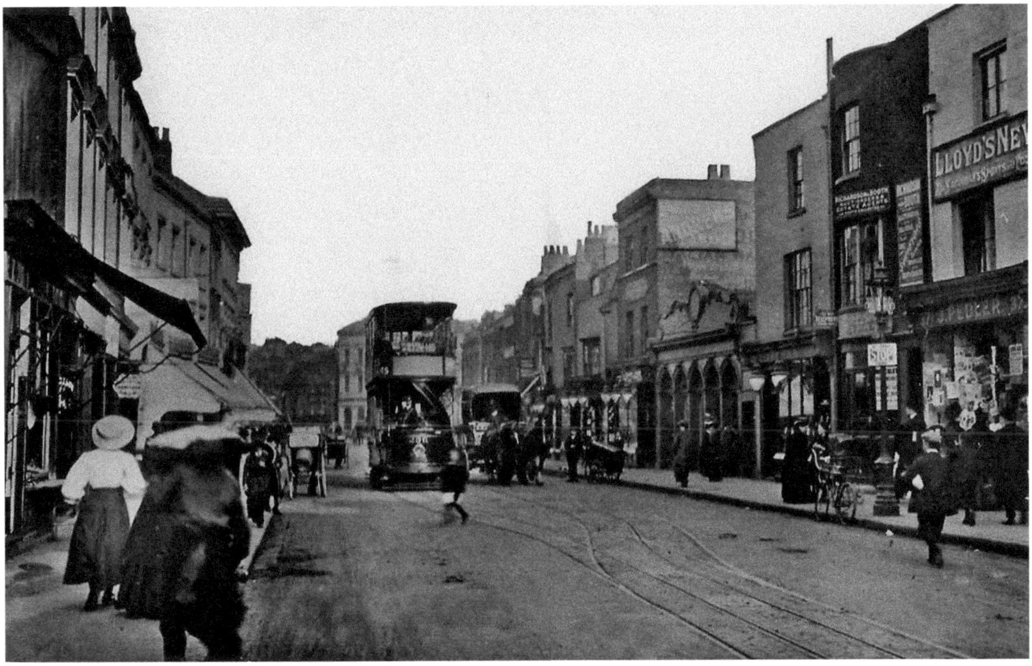


Tram traveling along London Street, now Greenwich South Street, early 1900s. Although trams were mostly powered by electricity, unsuccessful attempts were made to power horseless trams by steam and compressed air.

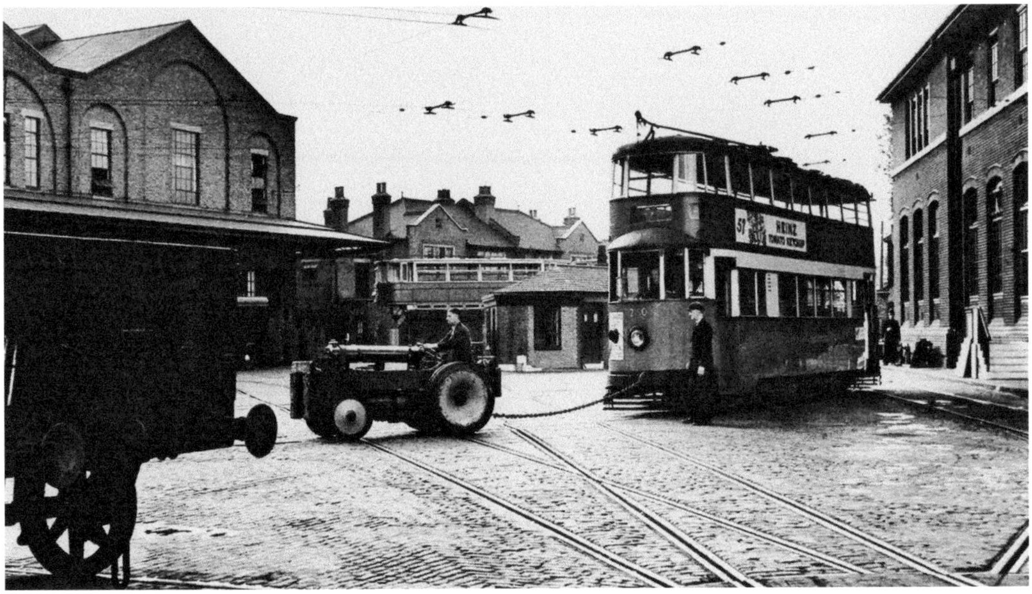


When the days of trams came to an end many went to Charlton for breaking up. There were two Charlton tram depots: a refurbishment and maintenance yard at Felltram Way, which later became an Airfix model-making factory, and the breakers' yard at Pelham Way, close to the Thames Barrier. (Greenwich Heritage Centre)

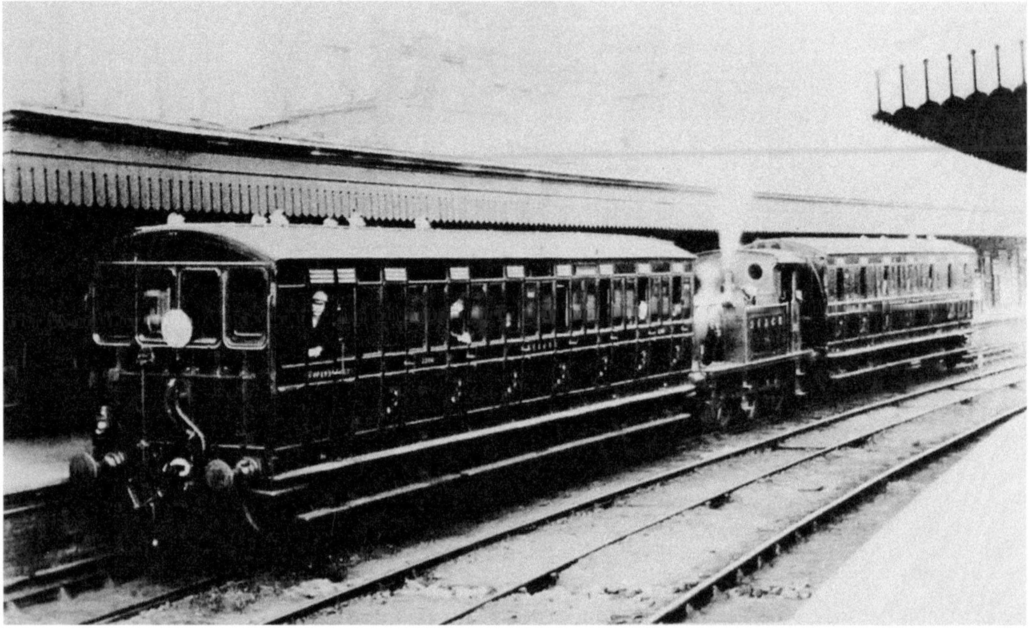

Sandwich passenger train, with the steam locomotive at the centre. Greenwich Park Station, *c.* 1910.

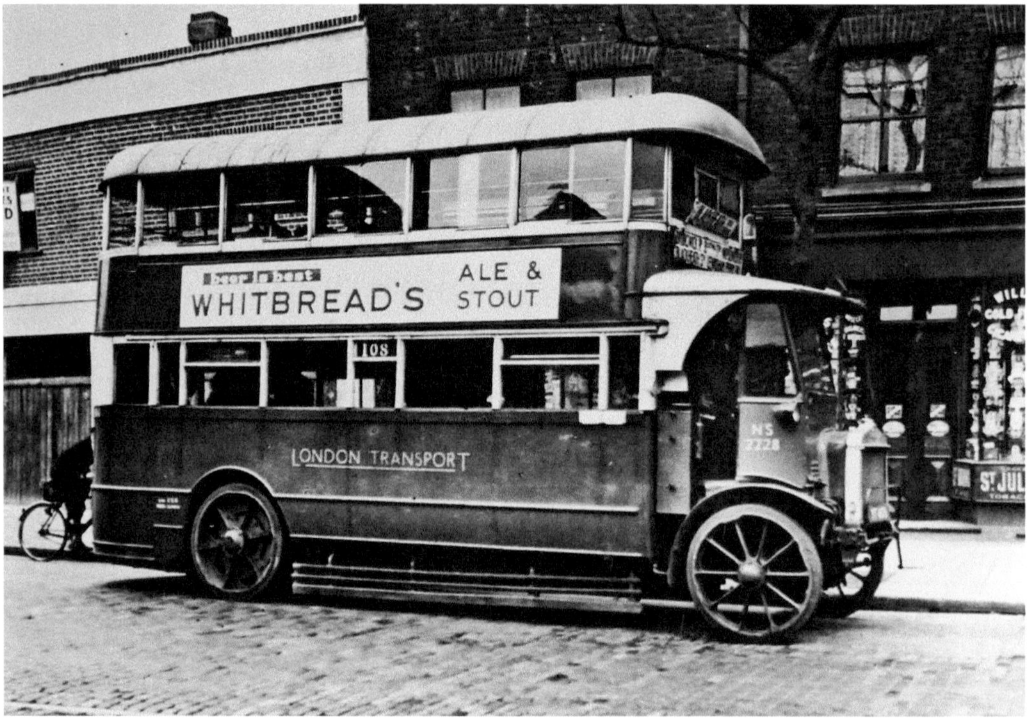


London Transport motor bus, route 108, which commenced operation in 1914, running between Bow Bridge, East London, to Blackheath via the Blackwall Tunnel.

# INTO THE TWENTY-FIRST CENTURY

Although the whole river frontage stretching from Deptford to Greenwich then onwards to Woolwich suffered from Second World War bombing raids during the Blitz, many long-established local businesses survived, the damaged buildings, wharfs and jetties repaired to allow work to carry on as normal. It would not be long, however, before the survivors of Greenwich's working and industrial past gradually succumbed to the passage of time.

Up until the mid-1900s you would still be able to find a few remaining Greenwich bombsites, which were local children's adventure playgrounds of the day, but these would soon be built upon, usually with plainly designed blocks of residential properties or unattractive prefabricated industrial buildings and storage units. As the riverside and Greenwich Marsh-based trades and industries fell into a gradual decline, some relocating while others closed altogether, the working practices of the local community were affected by a shift from industry and manufacturing to sales and retail, resulting in a planned regeneration programme for Greenwich leading towards the second millennium.

## INDUSTRIAL TRANSFORMATION

After the building of the Millennium Dome, rebranded the O2 Arena in 2005, and following on from the millennium celebrations, the exhibition space, along with 170 acres of redundant land, was placed up for sale in a plan to revitalise the sparsely populated area of Greenwich Marsh, part of the proposed Thames Gateway, a government echo-region initiative.

The scheme was conceived to supplement the local council's own regeneration plans, both sides of the river, to alleviate the population growth pressures of London and the South East, and support 'green' economic developments. Greenwich Peninsula was earmarked for the building of over 15,000 new homes, a design district, entertainment venues, shopping outlets, leisure and sports facilities, hotels, restaurants and education facilities, resulting in an expected creation of around 13,000 jobs.

To the south of the old Gasometer, the only reminder of the former Greenwich Gas Works, is the low carbon district energy centre, its advanced boiler technology saving up to 20,000 tons of carbon annually while generating electricity and producing heat and hot water to supply new properties erected across the peninsula. The rectangular energy complex comprises of

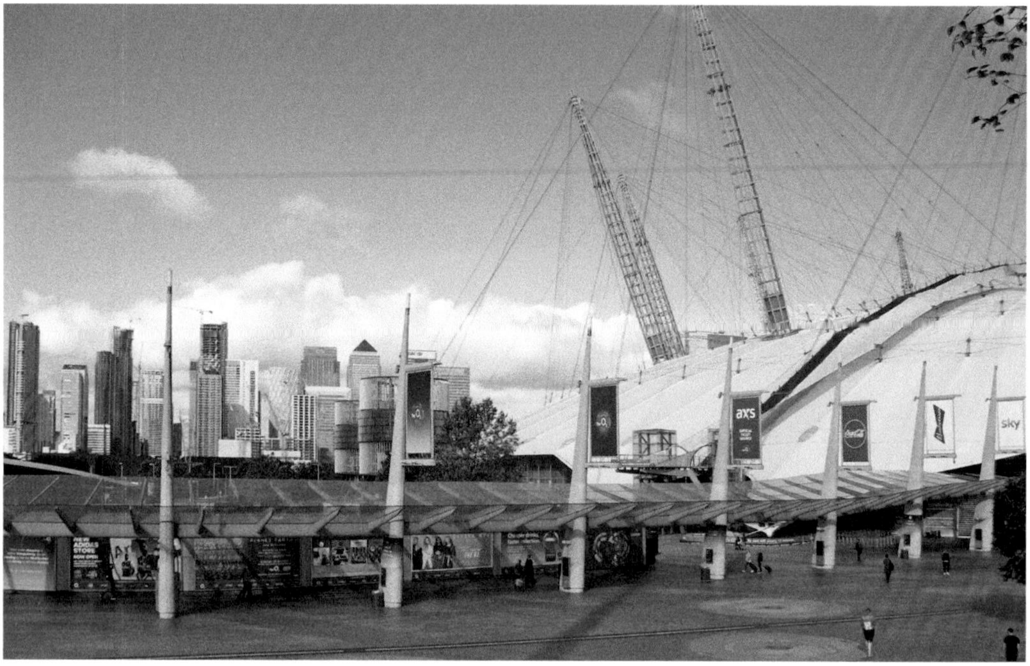


The highly successful entertainments venue the O2 Arena, originally built for the 2000 millennium celebrations.

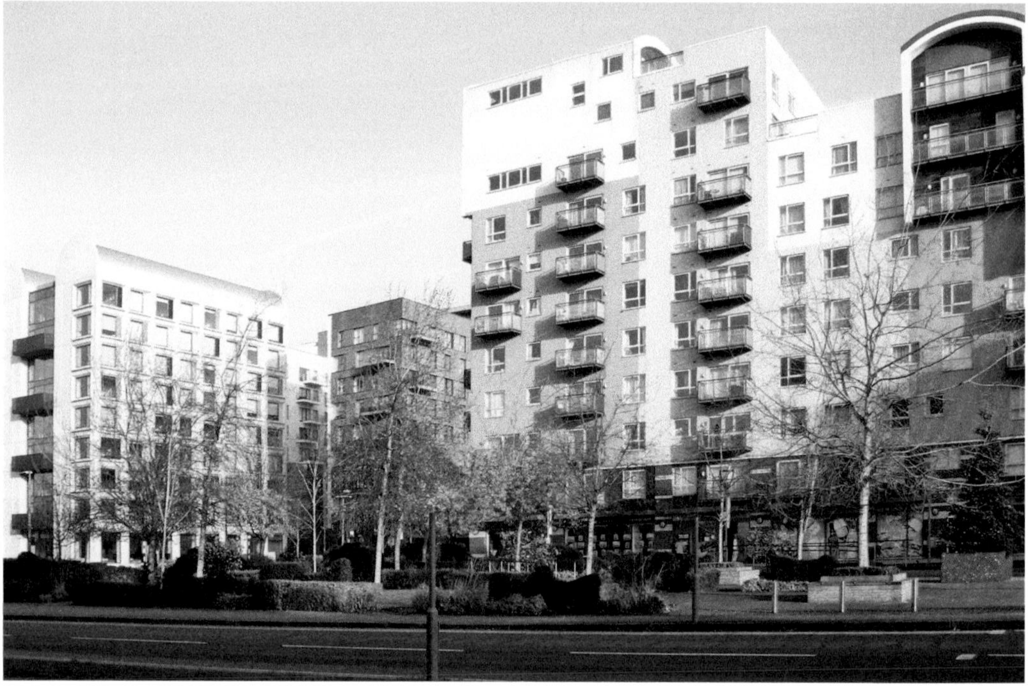

New modern residential apartments erected to the east of Greenwich Marsh, renamed Greenwich Peninsula.

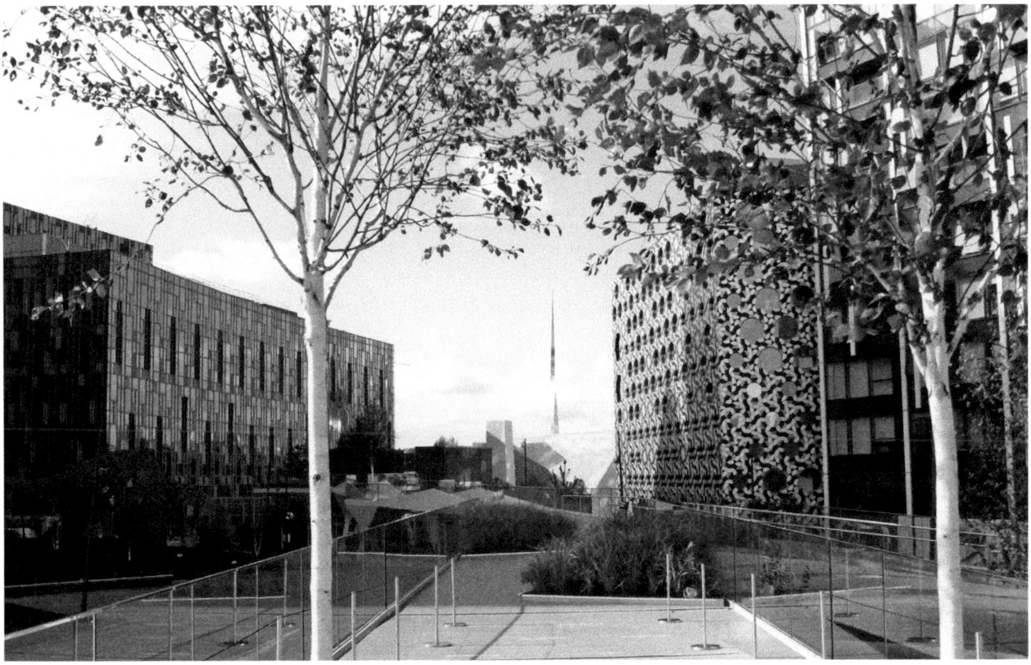

The Tide, London's first elevated riverside linear park, running from Peninsula Square to the river, will eventually encompass the whole peninsula.

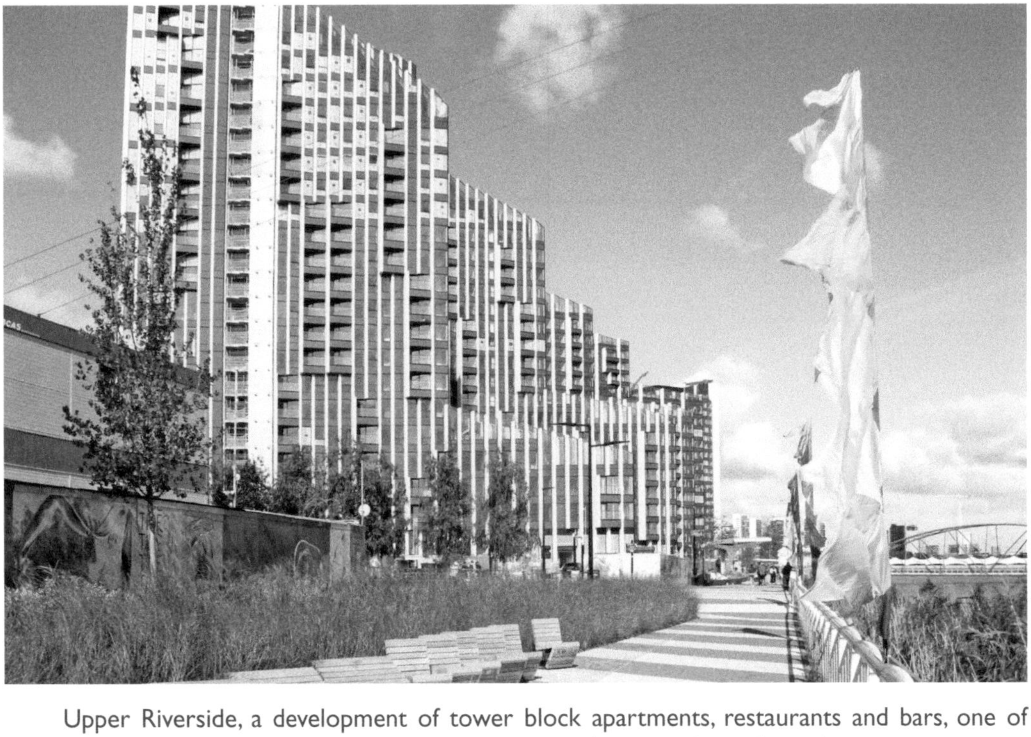

Upper Riverside, a development of tower block apartments, restaurants and bars, one of seven new neighbourhoods to be built across the former industrial marsh.

a substation, gas governor house, interactive educational visitor centre, offices and a striking 49-metre-high architectural flue stack, the Optic Cloak, illuminated at night from within, its sculptured geometric surface based upon First World War ships' dazzle camouflage.

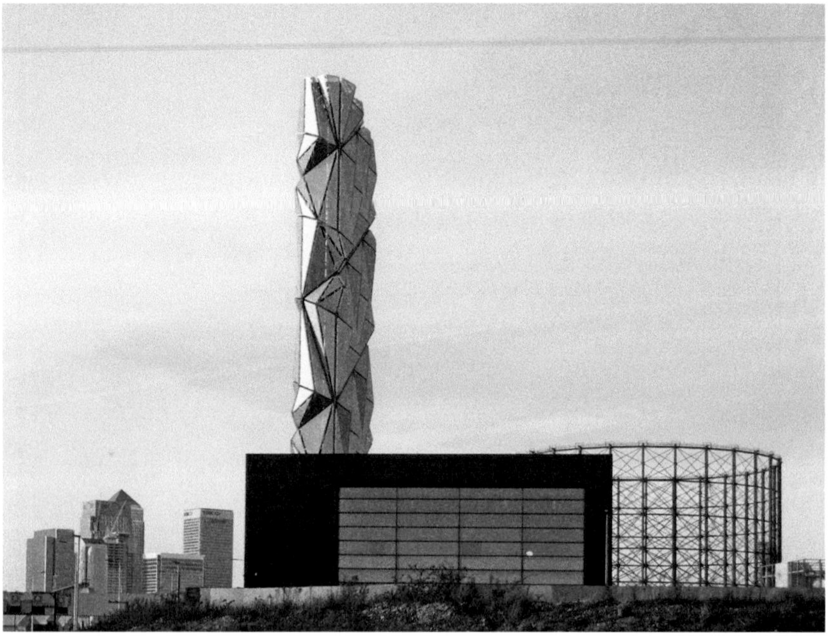

Low Carbon District Energy Centre, completed in 2017.

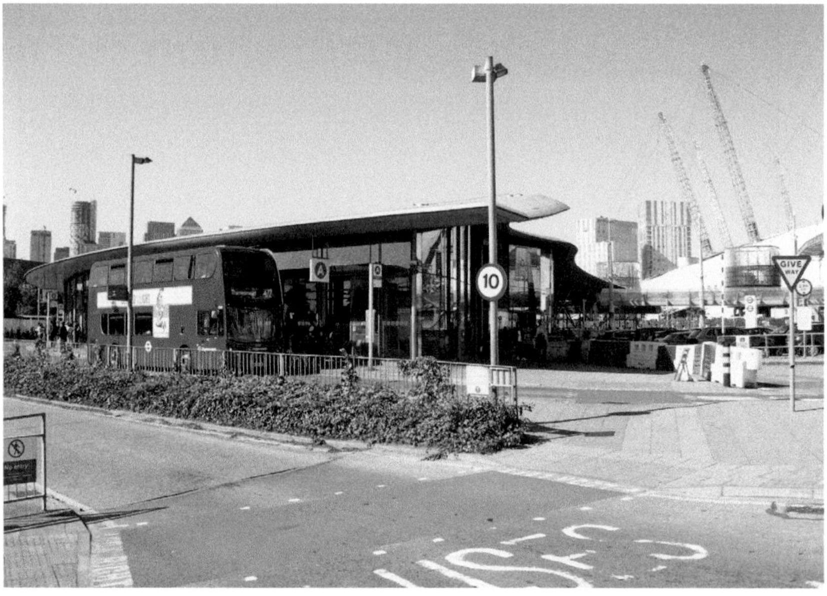


North Greenwich underground and bus station. Presented with an architectural award leading up to the new millennium, the transport complex serves residents and commuters across the whole of Greenwich.

# A NEW AGE FOR COMMUTER TRAVEL

The many new residents relocating to Greenwich Peninsula are now served by an integrated transport system, North Greenwich tube and bus station, North Greenwich Pier, and the Emirates Air Line, a cable car crossing the river to the Royal Victoria Dock and ExCel Exhibition Centre, another area of mass regeneration.

The London Underground station at North Greenwich, adjacent to the O2 Arena, is one of the largest on the Jubilee line, which at peak times is capable of managing around 20,000 passengers an hour, travellers including tourists, O2 Arena audiences and commuters. Although the low-profile-designed building received the RIBA Award 1999, there are ongoing plans to refurbish or even rebuild the station as part of a new £1billion property development.

From the station buses run on routes to Stratford, Greenwich Town Centre, Blackheath, Charlton, Woolwich, Thamesmead, Chislehurst, Bexleyheath, Lewisham and Central London. During 2018, it was estimated an average of 39,500 passengers used the bus services at North Greenwich every day. North Greenwich Pier, formally known as QEII Pier in honour of Queen Elizabeth II, was originally a coal jetty, which was demolished apart from eight cast-iron caisson columns, retained to secure the ultra-modern floating pier used by the Thames Clipper service.

Thames Clippers run commuter and passenger services from Tilbury to Putney, stopping off at piers located each side of the river, including Woolwich Royal Arsenal, North Greenwich and Greenwich Cutty Sark. The majority of these sleekly designed vessels are twin-hulled catamarans, the fleet transporting approximately 8,500 passengers each day. With a staff of almost 400, further expansion to the river service will include new, larger catamarans and ferries taking cruise liner passengers into central London from ships moored downriver.

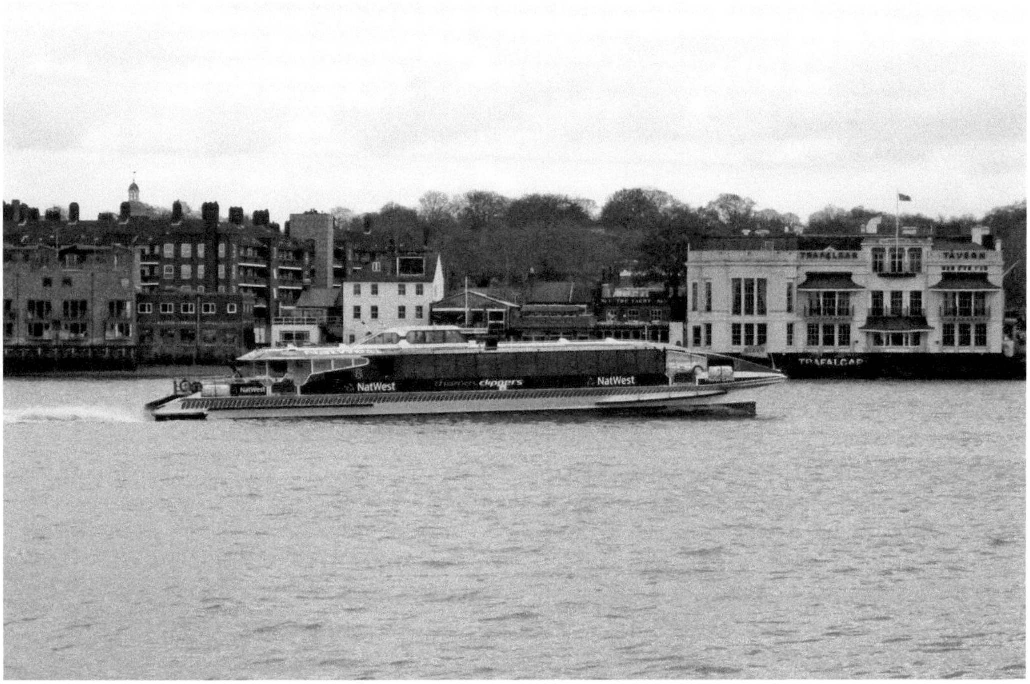


Thames Clipper catamaran passing the historic Trafalgar Tavern at Greenwich Reach.

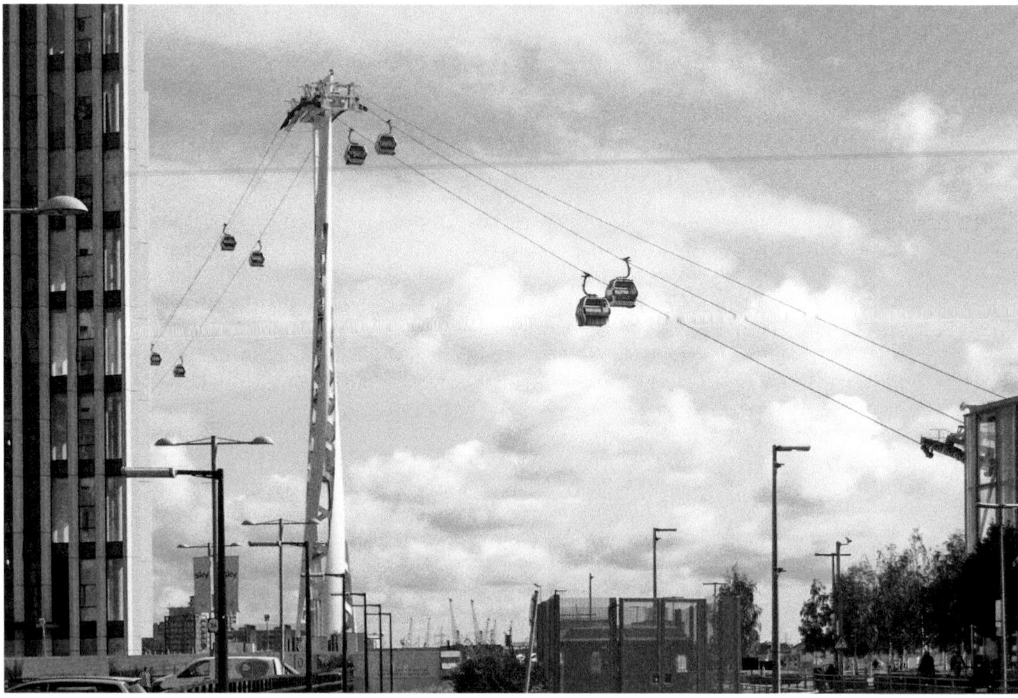

Emirates Airline, a cable car service taking passengers across the Thames from Greenwich to Royal Victoria Dock.

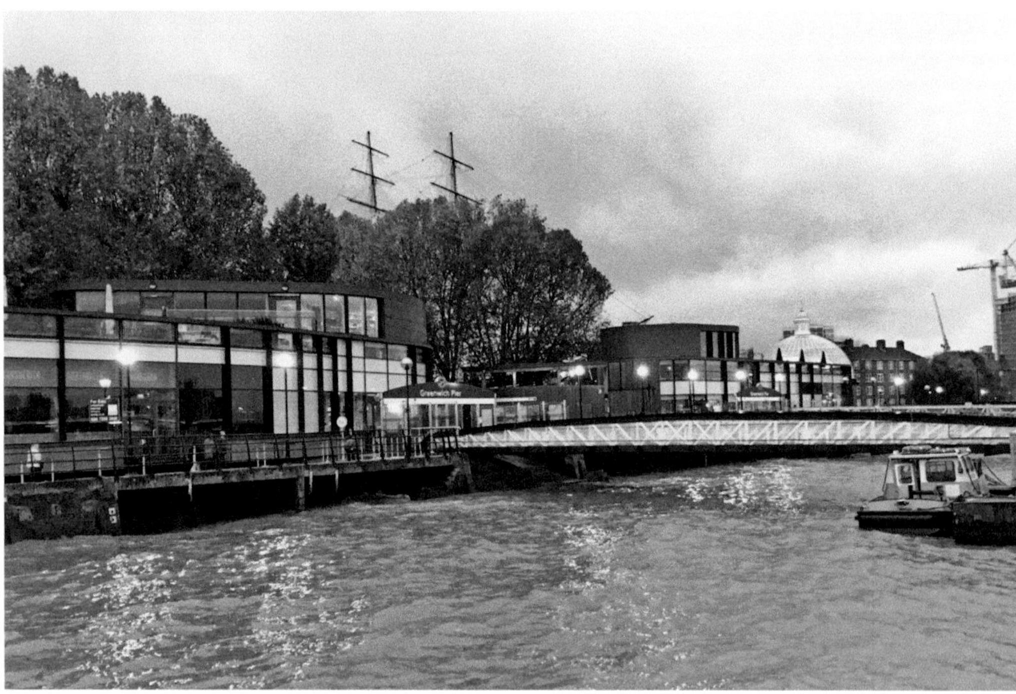

Greenwich Pier, refurbished in time for the London Olympics 2012.

When the Emirates Air Line cable car opened in June 2012, it was projected that 2,500 passengers could be carried in each direction every hour. The hope was the service would operate to maximum capacity during peak hours when commuters travelled to and from their places of work. The thirty-four gondolas travel 1,100 metres across the river at a height of up to 90 metres, each one carrying a maximum of ten passengers, the cables supported by three spiral pylons. The crossing, or flight as the journey is described, takes between five to ten minutes, depending on the time of day passengers travel, as the gondolas travel faster during commuter rush hours.

There are two Air Line pavilions, one situated each side of the Thames. The Greenwich pavilion includes a large gondola garage and service workshop, ticket office, café and the Emirates Aviation Experience, a state-of-the-art interactive commercial airline exhibition, including four aircraft flight simulators for visitors to try out their piloting skills. Unfortunately, the cable car service failed to attract the number of commuters as expected, although many tourists take trips across the river, especially during the summer months.

It has been estimated that just over 28,000 passengers travelled on the cable car during 2018, and with ongoing plans to build more new residential properties both sides of the river, along with the expansion of new business and leisure facilities creating a growth in employment opportunities, the cable car service may well carry many more passengers annually than it has done previously.

Although many of the regeneration projects across the Peninsula and along the river frontage from Deptford to Woolwich are predominantly residential, new community neighbourhoods replacing the old working districts, the Royal Borough of Greenwich planned to transform the local economy by attracting progressive modern businesses into the area, which, in turn, would create new job opportunities for local people.

## MODERNISATION OF A TRADITIONAL INDUSTRY

Like many small towns during the industrial age, brewing had once been an important local industry. However, when large national breweries began buying up small independent brewers and then obtaining ownership of a chain of public houses, the Greenwich brewing trade finally came to an end in 1959, when Lovibonds turned its business interests towards the wine trade rather than beer. Then, at the turn of the twenty-first century, Alastair Hook, postgraduate in brewing and biochemistry, founded the Meantime Brewery and began brewing beer in a small unit on a Charlton industrial estate. So successful was this microbrewery that within ten years Meantime Brewery moved into a new £2 million Moeschle brewery on Blackwall Lane.

Employing up to 100 staff, the Meantime Brewery produces around 120,000 hectolitres of ales, lagers and speciality beers annually. These brews are sold locally and nationally, and at the brewery's onsite bar and restaurant. The Meantime Brewery is just one of almost 12,000 businesses in the borough, a commercial service sector which includes information technology, communications, retail, tourism and creative and digital industries linked to Ravensbourne University.

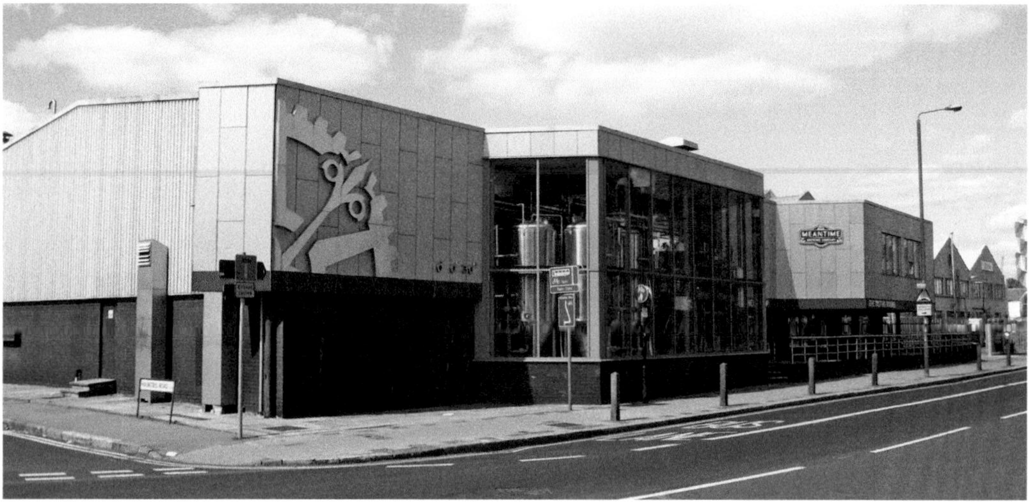


Meantime's state-of-the-art brewery, bar and restaurant on Blackwall Lane.

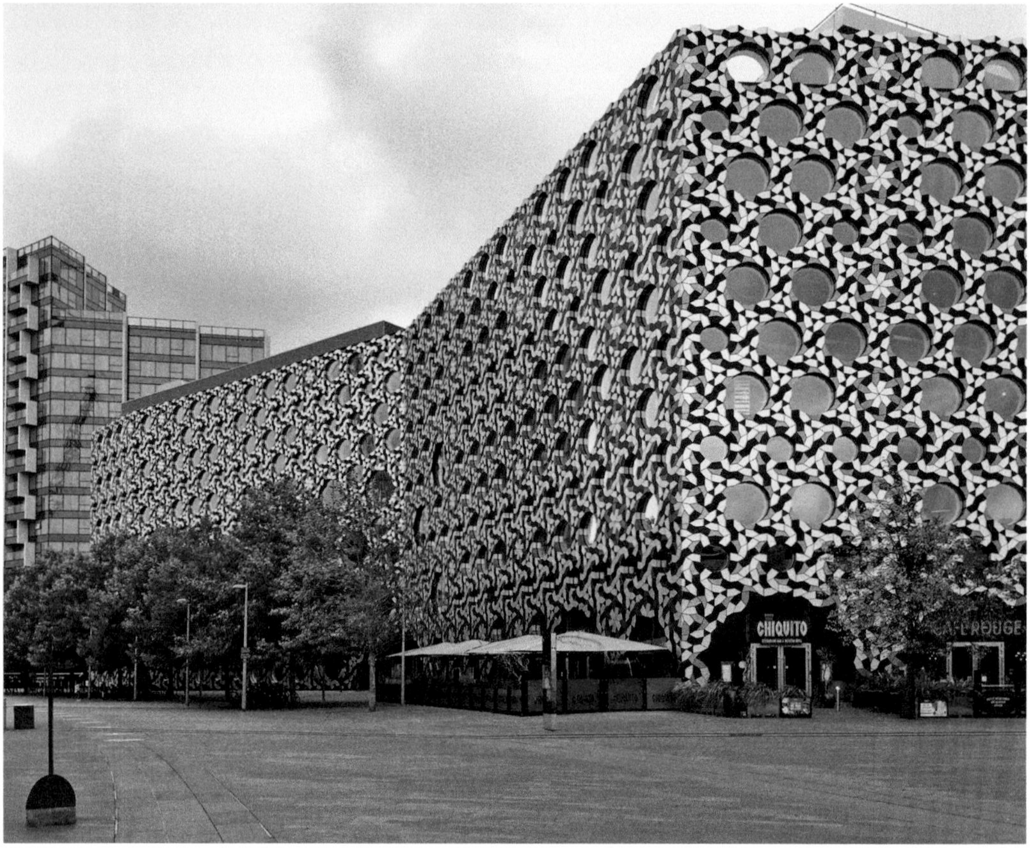


Ravensbourne University, to the south of the O2 Arena, a single faculty split into various design departments, employs approximately 140 academic staff and currently has 2,400 undergraduate and postgraduate students.

# EDUCATING ENTREPRENEURS, DESIGNERS AND ARTISTS PAST, PRESENT AND FUTURE

After Ravensbourne College for Design and Communications outgrew its campus at Chislehurst, a new site was obtained at the heart of the Greenwich Peninsula Business Centre, close to the O2, to build a futuristic four-storey educational facility. The building, clad in 28,000 mathematically patterned anodised aluminium tiles and inset with circular glazed windows, was completed in the summer of 2010, at a cost of £70 million, and by 2018 Ravensbourne had received university status.

Alongside the education of students, Ravensbourne hosts over 100 creative technology businesses utilising the university's design and media resources. Working in close collaboration with prospective employers, university students are provided with the practical skills creative industries require from graduates.

To the west of Greenwich is another new education building: the library and academic centre of the University of Greenwich. After the Royal Navy moved out of the Royal Naval College during the late 1900s, several of the college's historic buildings were acquired by the University of Greenwich. Founded in 1891 as the Woolwich Polytechnic, the education facility obtained university status in 1991.

There are now three campuses – Medway, Avery Hill and Greenwich – and as the university expanded its educational programmes, covering subjects including architecture, business, computing, mathematics, engineering, humanities, maritime studies, natural sciences, pharmaceuticals and social sciences, a new building was opened at Stockwell Street in 2014, to house an extensive collection of books and journals. Along with the library, the building also accommodates departments of architecture and landscape design, digital arts and various other creative professions. The ground floor, accessed by students and the public, includes a lecture theatre, exhibition areas, café, print shop and legal advice centre.

Renowned graduates of the University of Greenwich, and the former polytechnic, include 2009 Nobel Prize winner for Physics Charles Kao, awarded for his work on the transmission of light through fibre optics; British Aerospace and BAE Systems board member and businessman George Rose; former Chief Executive of Formula One Group and business magnet Bernie Ecclestone; and a host of distinguished authors, artists, actors and musicians.

Within the former Royal Naval College, alongside the University of Greenwich, is the Trinity Laban Conservatoire of Music and Dance, formed in 2005 through a merger between Trinity College of Music, founded in 1872, and the Laban Dance Centre, founded as the Art of Movement Studio in 1948.

The conservatoire is recognised internationally as a leading school for music and dance training, with just over 1,000 undergraduate and postgraduate students, and comprises of performers, composers and choreographers and around 600 staff, including teachers, artists, researchers and support staff, all spread across its three campuses – Deptford, New Cross and Greenwich.

During interior refurbishment of the Royal Naval College building, to provide new recital rooms, it was discovered the original Greenwich Hospital structure had incorporated masonry from the Tudor royal palace, demolished during the seventeenth century, a period in time when Greenwich was emerging as a significant and important centre of industry.

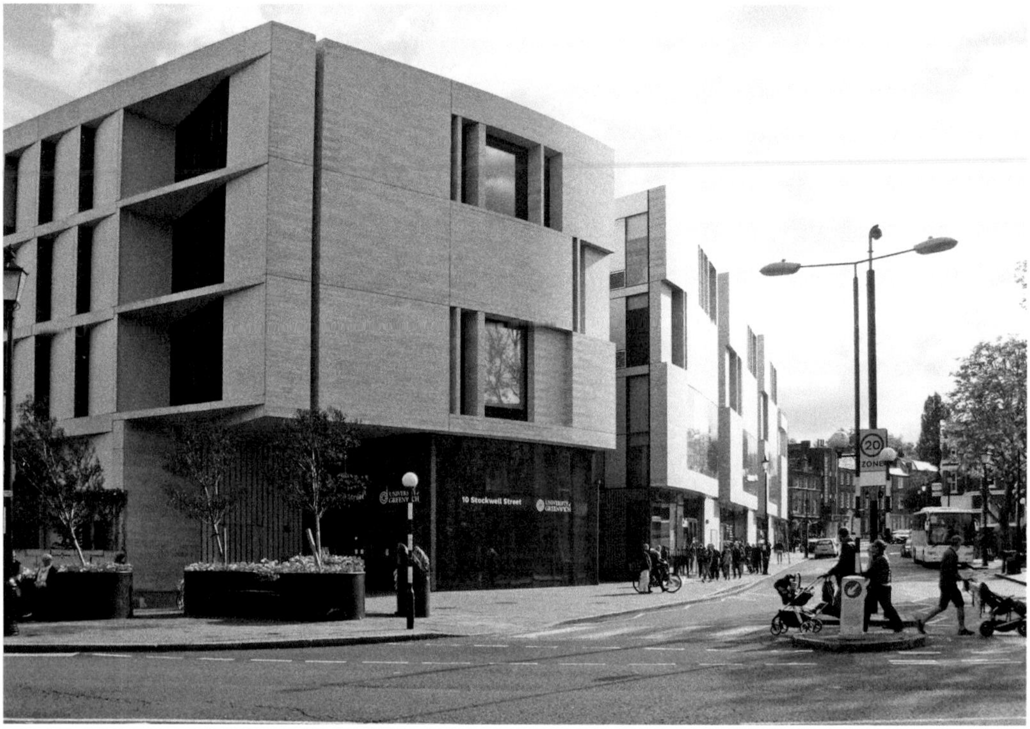


University of Greenwich Stockwell Street campus. The final design included limestone cladding to complement the classical styles of surrounding historic buildings.

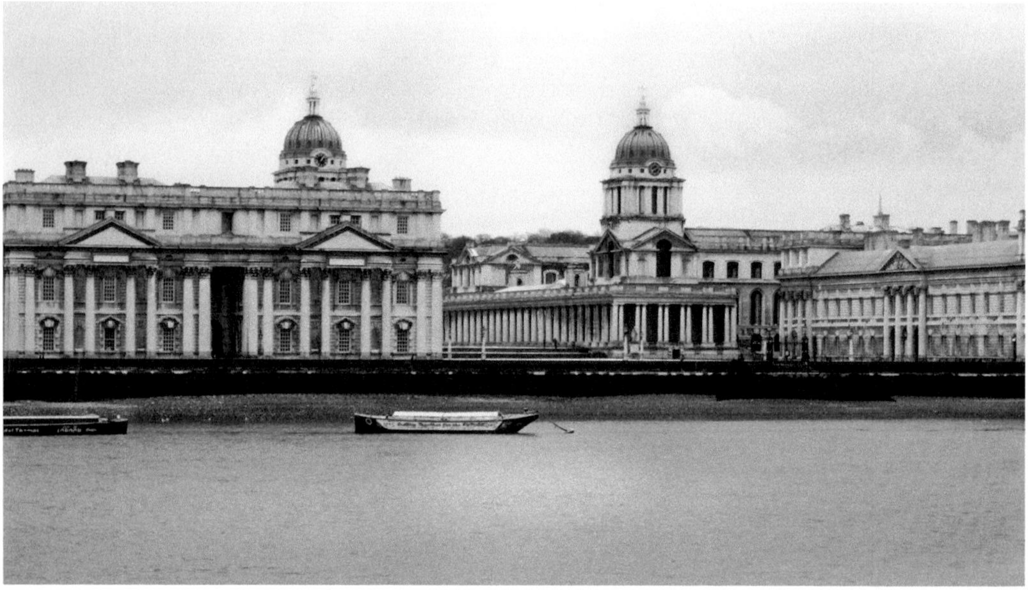

The Old Royal Naval College is now home to the University of Greenwich and Trinity Laban Conservatoire of Music and Dance. The historic painted hall, chapel and grounds are open to the public.

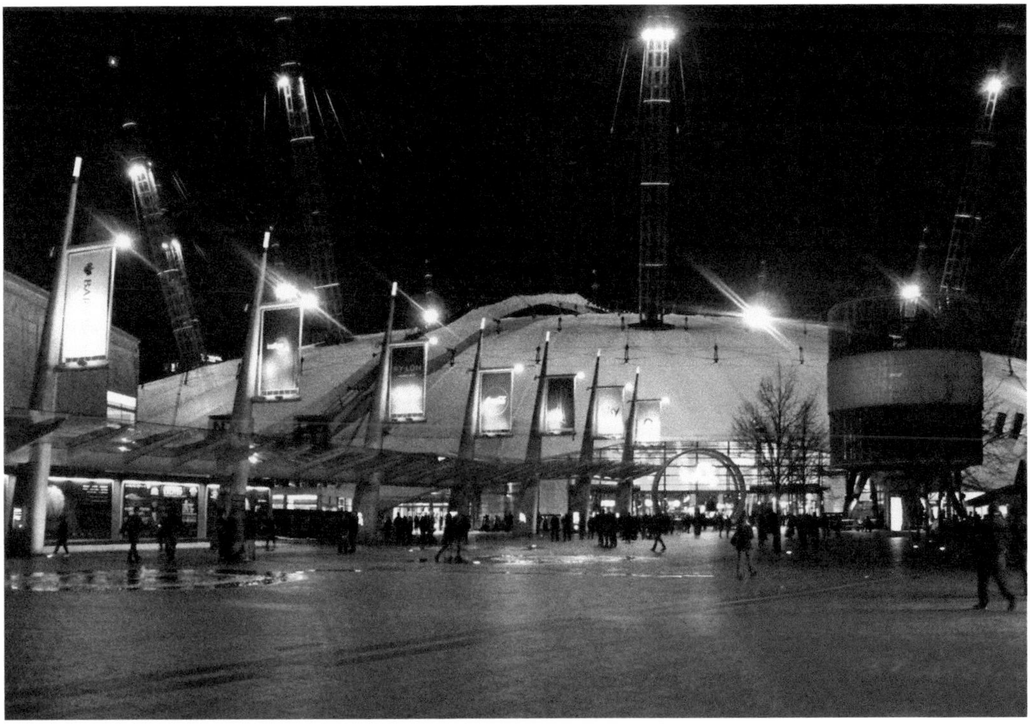

Greenwich Peninsula, the O2 and Creative Design District, 2020.

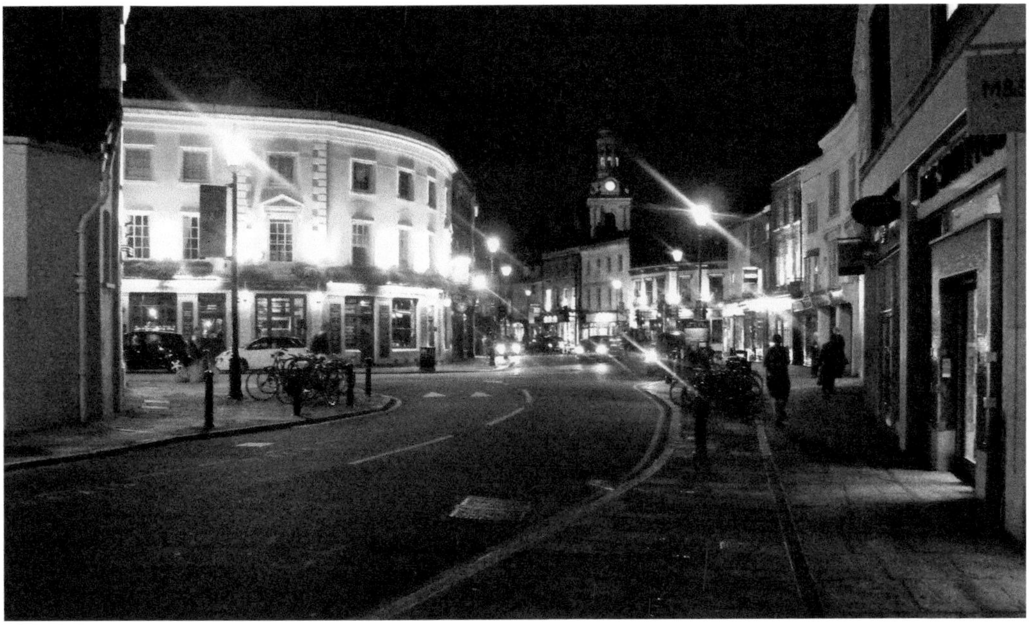

Once a busy and bustling place of work and trade, the town centre of Greenwich has become a popular and attractive tourist destination, with boutique shops, bars, restaurants and many places of historic interest and importance.

# BIBLIOGRAPHY

Ed., Armstrong, Alan, *The Economy of Kent 1640-1914* (Suffolk, Boydell Press, 1995), Jerrold, Walter, *Highways and Byways of Kent* (Macmillan, 1907), Ed., Kelly, E. R., *Kelly's Directory of Kent* (London, Kelly & Co., 1882), Ed., Weinreb, Ben and Hibbert, Christopher, *The London Encyclopaedia* (Pan MacMillan, 1983) Websites:- Ancestry, Barge Trust, British History Online, GMT 2000, Greenwich Industrial History Society, Merryweather and Son Ltd, Oxford Bibliographies, Proceedings of The Old Bailey, Thames Police Association, Victorian Web and Vision of Britain.

# ACKNOWLEDGEMENTS

The author and publisher would like to thank the following for assistance in the research for this publication: British Library, Caird Library & Archive National Maritime Museum, Greenwich Heritage Centre, Lovibonds Brewery, Meantime Brewery, National Archive, Old Royal Naval College, Royal Parks and University of Greenwich. Photographs supplied by A. Phinbow, image 16; Greenwich Heritage Centre, images 3, 15, 32, 42, 46, 57, 94, 108, 111, 127; Lovibonds Brewery, image 96; Roger Cooper, image 122, and the many retailors at postcard fairs and antiquarian shops who have assisted me in locating images and photographs used in this publication. If for any reason I have not accredited people or organisations as necessary, or used copyright material without permission/acknowledgement, I apologise for any oversight and will make the necessary correction at the first opportunity.

Special thanks to Greenwich residents Roger Cooper and Peter Andrews, for providing local history information, and to the family members of my distant cousin Audrey Mills, and Ramzan, Pearce and Peachey family members who, over the years, have provided both family and local history information, as well as many photographs included within *Greenwich at Work*.

# ABOUT THE AUTHOR

Born in Greenwich, London, David Ramzan has always had a keen interest in the history of his home town and studied local history at the University of Oxford. A self-employed graphic designer, illustrator and artist, he also works in special needs education and has written several historical publications and articles for magazines and periodicals, subjects including local town and maritime history, football, smuggling and Victorian crime.